Springer Series on Social Work

Albert R. Roberts, Ph.D., Series Editor
Graduate School of Social Work, Rutgers,
The State University of New Jersey

1984 **Clinical Social Work in Health Settings:** A Guide to Professional Practice with Exemplars, *Thomas Owen Carlton, D.S.W.*

1987 **Information and Referral Networks:** Doorways to Human Services, *Risha W. Levinson, D.S.W.*

1988 **Social Work in the Workplace:** Practice and Principles, *Gary M. Gould, Ph.D., and Michael Lane Smith, Ph.D.*

1990 **Social Work Practice in Maternal and Child Health,** *Terri Combs-Orme, Ph.D.*

1990 **Program Evaluation in the Human Services,** *Michael J. Smith, D.S.W.*

1990 **Evaluating Your Practice:** A Guide to Self-Assessment, *Catherine Alter, Ph.D., and Wayne Evens, M.S.W.*

1990 **Violence Hits Home:** Comprehensive Treatment Approaches to Domestic Violence, *Sandra M. Stith, Ph.D., Mary Beth Williams, Ph.D., and Karen Rosen, M.S.*

1991 **Breast Cancer in the Life Course:** Women's Experiences, *Julianne S. Oktay, Ph.D., and Carolyn Ambler Walter, Ph.D.*

1991 **Victimization and Survivor Services:** A Guide to Victim Assistance, *Arlene Bowers Andrews, Ph.D.*

1992 **The Family Functioning Scale:** A Guide to Research and Practice, *Ludwig L. Geismar, Ph.D., and Michael Camasso, Ph.D.*

1994 **Dilemmas in Human Services Management:** Illustrative Case Studies, *Raymond Sanchez Mayers, Ph.D., Federico Souflee, Jr., Ph.D., and Dick J. Schoech, Ph.D.*

1994 **Managing Work and Family Life,** *Viola M. Lechner, D.S.W., and Michael A. Creedon, D.S.W.*

1996 **Total Quality Management in Human Service Organizations,** *John J. Gunther, D.S.W., and Frank Hawkins, D.S.W.*

John J. Gunther, DSW, is a professor, director, and MSW coordinator for the School of Social Work at Southwest Missouri State University. Prior to his current leadership position, he was director of the social work program at Southeastern Louisiana University. He has been a member of the graduate faculty at Southern University–New Orleans and Tulane University and on the doctoral faculty at Tulane. Previously, he has chaired the Administration, Planning, and Social Policy sequences for graduate and undergraduate education at Southern University–New Orleans and the University of Oklahoma. Dr. Gunther has chaired the Quality Management Committee of the Louisiana Health Care campaign and has served on the Quality Assurance Committee for the State of Louisiana in their design of a statewide TQM system for health care. He is an active member of the American Society of Quality Control. Nationally, Dr. Gunther has been chair of NASW-PACE and an NASW representative to the Delegate Assembly. Dr. Gunther has been a management consultant and presenter on TQM both nationally and internationally.

Frank Hawkins, DSW, is a professor at Memorial University of Newfoundland in St. John's, Newfoundland, Canada, where he has been a faculty member in the School of Social Work since 1970. He served as Director of the School of Social Work from 1984–1989. Since 1994 he has been chair of Memorial's Ph.D. studies program in social work. His teaching and research interests are in the areas of social policy, management education, and organizational development. He is a former President of the Canadian Association of Schools of Social Work. Dr. Hawkins holds undergraduate degrees from Memorial University of Newfoundland, an MSW from the University of Toronto, and a DSW from Tulane University. He has worked as a management consultant and trainer in Canada, the United States, Great Britain, and Japan.

Making TQM Work

Quality Tools
For Human Service Organizations

John Gunther, DSW
Frank Hawkins, DSW

 Springer Publishing Company

Springer Publishing Company, Inc.
536 Broadway
New York, NY 10012-3955

Cover design by Janet Joachim
Acquisitions Editor: Bill Tucker
Production Editor: Jeanne Libby

99 00 01 02 03 / 5 4 3 2 1

Library of Congress Cataloging-in-Publication Data

Gunther, John Joseph, 1946–
    Making TQM work : quality tools for human service organizations /
by John Gunther and Frank Hawkins.
       p. cm. — (Springer series on social work)
    Includes bibliographical references.
    ISBN 0-8261-1187-4 (softcover)
    1. Total quality management in human services. I. Hawkins,
Frank. II. Title III. Series.
HV41.G95   1999
361'.0068'5—dc21   98-56533
                                              CIP

Printed in the United States of America

Contents

To Jeanette and Celeste

Foreword

Total Quality Management is relatively new to the field of human services. In less than two decades the central tenets of TQM have challenged the management thinking of decision makers in all sectors of the corporate world. However, it has only been in this decade, the nineties, that we have seen writers in the field of human services management examine the relevance and applicability of this new paradigm to the concerns facing not-for-profit organizations. Gunther and Hawkins (1996) were among the first writers to illustrate the relevance of TQM to human service organizations. In their text *Total Quality Management in Human Service Organizations* they gave profile to the need for service providers to reexamine their commitment to customers in the provision of quality services. They drew from the work of key management theorists, including Deming, Crosby, and Juran and outlined the essential components of a model to effectively implement TQM in human service organizations. The efficacy and application of this model is seen in a variety of practice settings where TQM has been adopted. Their case studies provided the reader with in-depth description and analysis on how quality became the driving force to organizational change and service improvement. Now the authors have taken us a step further in their new book *Making TQM Work: Quality Tools for Human Service Organizations.*

This book is a logical sequel to their first book in that here the emphasis is on skill development. While there is ample discussion and analysis of the theory behind quality management, the focus here is on the skills needed to effectively address quality problems in the workplace, particularly the world of "non-profits." Skills are brought to life in a series of experiential exercises which draw the reader into the actual tasks inherent in problem solving "quality issues." The emphasis is on understanding and learning key skills that are fundamental to a successful TQM initiative. The reader is introduced to a variety of quality tools which cross a spectrum of management tasks.

It is quickly apparent to the reader that this text is different. This is not a quick fix to organizational problems. Consistent with the TQM philosophy of the need for pervasive organizational change, this book provides insight into the myriad of "processes" that come under the scrutiny of practitioners who are committed to the realization of quality in all facets of organizational life. Thus, concepts such as employee empowerment, team building, customer needs assessment, quality training, organizational culture, quality costs, process control, continuous quality improvement and benchmarking are included in the "tool kit" of these authors who are serious about the "nuts and bolts" of what it takes to make TQM work.

As the authors indicate in this text, TQM has become an organizational imperative for human service delivery systems in this post-modern era. Measures of success in the field of health and social services in the new millennium will be largely dependent upon how the issue of "quality" is addressed in terms of outcome measures. The current realities of an increasingly competitive work environment and the global economy make this an issue that cannot be avoided if we are to rise to the challenges of our rapidly changing social and economic marketplace.

Gunther and Hawkins have produced a text which builds upon the realities of a shift in management thinking, a paradigm shift, which demands critical changes at all levels of organizational life in the interest of quality initiatives. While this text will not solve all our problems, it makes an important contribution in outlining and operationalizing the skills needed to make quality a reality in human service organizations. This is not viewed as an individual effort, rather it is seen as the product of professionals working together in a shared commitment to continuous quality improvement. Springer Publishing Company is to be commended for bringing this important book to market. It is indeed timely, and presents a challenge to all of us to make "quality" a synergistic reality in the workplace.

WILLIAM ROWE, DSW
Director and Professor
McGill University
School of Social Work

Preface

This textbook and the accompanying experiential exercises were written to enhance the knowledge and skill base of human service managers of the various "tools" used in total quality management (TQM). The major focus of this book is the application and implementation of TQM tools. The major purpose for writing this text is to fill a substantive gap that appears within the human service organization literature. This book provides help in the application of quality tools in human service organizations as they relate to problem identification, problem analysis, problem solving, decision making, customer satisfaction, team building, and work processes. Educationally, this book is meant to teach both undergraduate and graduate students the skills needed to engage in effective and efficient quality management. The worksheets accompanying the experiential exercises are meant to serve as a means to understanding the practice skills needed to become a total quality manager. Instructors who use the book in their classrooms will find it invaluable in the development of organizational and management skills. Classroom role playing, skill development, and reflective or intuitive understanding of the material serve as the organizing framework for students to become proficient practitioners. This text complements the text *Total Quality Management in the Human Services* (Gunther & Hawkins, 1996), and when used together they support a fully integrated approach to the effective implementation of TQM.

Previous work (Gunther & Hawkins, 1996; Ginsberg & Keys, 1996; Martin, 1993; and Edwards, Yankey, & Altpeter, 1998) on the implementation of TQM in the human services has focused on developing an organizational culture of quality and building a foundation supported by specific quality premises. These premises are

- customer focus
- fact-based decision making
- continuous quality improvement
- process orientation

The literature has given extensive attention to the customer focus of TQM as a central tenet. The importance of analyzing organizational processes through teamwork and the promotion of a continuous quality improvement cycle has also received attention. The business literature has covered this topic extensively. In contrast, there has been a paucity of information on the importance and use of quality improvement tools in human service organizations. Current texts on this subject present the tools of quality improvement in outline form. They do not give profile to the day-to-day problems faced by professionals in human service organizations and the relevance and application of these tools to specific problems, however. In addition, current texts do not provide the reader with opportunities to work experientially with quality tools to achieve personal mastery in their use. The text *Making TQM Work: Tools for Human Service Organizations* addresses these gaps by introducing, describing, and explaining TQM tools and illustrating their application in human service organizations with case examples. Experiential exercises follow the case examples to reinforce the learning skills associated with the application of the tools.

Finally, three questions that every quality professional should ask (SAS Institute, 1996) are addressed and anchor each of the experiential exercises on TQM tools. These questions are as follows:

1. What happened?
2. Why did it happen?
3. What will happen next?

By addressing these questions, human service organizations can operationalize their commitment to quality services and take the first steps on the journey toward continuous quality improvement and the development of organizational cultures of quality.

REFERENCES

Edwards, R. L., Yankey, J. A., & Altpeter, M. A. (1998). *Skills for effective management of nonprofit organizations*. Washington, DC: NASW Press.

Ginsberg, L., & Keys, P. (1996). *New management in the human services*. Washington, DC: NASW Press.

Gunther, J., & Hawkins, F. (1996). *Total quality management in human service organizations*. New York: Springer.

Martin, L. (1993). *Total quality management in human service organizations*. Newbury Park, CA: Sage.

SAS Institute. (1996, May). 3 questions every quality professional should ask. *Quality Progress*, p. 11.

Acknowledgments

This book is about quality management. However, the book would have never been completed without the patience, love, and support of our wives, Jeanette Gunther and Celeste Hawkins. Also Alan and Patti Russell who provided a place for the authors to work uninterrupted for the many hours needed to make this book a reality. Jim Gunther was also a strong generator of ideas about the book.

On the professional level, the authors want to acknowledge our common mentor, Dr. Margaret Campbell, former Dean of Tulane University–School of Social Work. Dr. Campbell was a strong and a positive teaching influence on the two authors when they were young doctoral hopefuls. Dean Millie Charles of Southern University at New Orleans is also acknowledged for the quality advice and wisdom she has demonstrated over the years to John. Donna Elia, Barbara Noel, and Bridet Ghaney lent invaluable secretarial support to this book. Their support and professionalism were invaluable throughout this entire work.

Jason Paul and Barbara DaCosta, our research assistants, are acknowledged for their hard work and support. Without their long hours of research the book would not have been brought to fruition.

Finally, the authors wish to acknowledge their students and colleagues who have throughout the years challenged the authors in their thinking and have always made the task of learning exciting, and truly a journey in continuous quality improvement.

Old Problems–New Solutions: Building Quality in the Workplace

This book is for you! That is, if you want to enter the world of creativity, innovation, and quality-driven services. This book is not meant simply to be read; rather, it is meant to be experienced. You might ask, however, what is so different about TQM; isn't this just another fad? Or, what difference does it make to me? I'm not a manager. Anyway, just what is TQM? Doesn't TQM involve a lot of statistical tools? I'm really intimidated by stuff involving mathematics and numbers. Besides, they really don't relate to the kind of problems I face at work every day! Sound familiar?

Whether you are a clinician, manager, educator, or trainer, these questions point to some very real challenges to the understanding and implementation of total quality management (TQM). This book was written to address just such questions and to make TQM relevant and meaningful to workers everywhere who are charged with the responsibilities associated with the provision of human services. The journey into TQM forces us to look at organizations and our workplace differently. It is time to begin that journey.

FIRST THE BAD NEWS

One only needs to look around to see that public human services are in a state of decline. The privatization of government services; the emergence of managed care and models of managed competition in the delivery of health, social, and education services; the gradual movement toward privatizing the social security system; and the outsourcing of human services are all patterns that reflect a new emphasis on the importance of cost efficiencies. Little attention is being given to considerations having to do with service quality. The following example illustrates the kinds of problems that currently exist. Recently in the town of Gander, Newfoundland, Canada, a nursing home decided to outsource its food services and close down its on-site kitchen facilities. The outsourcing was viewed by some to hold great promise, with a number of financial economies to be realized. The residents of the nursing home were very upset with the arrangement, however, so much so that they decided to call a media press conference to voice their dissatisfaction. The senior citizens were very unhappy with the "quality" of the food being transported to the home from a nearby hospital. An ensuing study indicated that the food was indeed nutritious. Nevertheless, the seniors were dissatisfied. They missed the smells of food preparation and the "homelike" atmosphere for dining that existed prior to the outsourcing of meals. Ultimately, the seniors were successful in having their on-site kitchen restored to the nursing home.

This case illustrates several key points essential to an understanding of TQM. Perhaps the most important lesson to be learned is that if customers (staff members or clients) are dissatisfied, it will cost the organization. Customer dissatisfaction will not only cost the organization financially but also cost in the wear and tear of personal stress and in the negativity and disillusionment coloring workplace relationships. Workers will not be giving their best. The net result will be poor quality with a gradual decrease in the levels of effective service, an increase in the incidence of staff "burn out," and open expressions of apathy about work and the workplace. Is this beginning to sound familiar? Does this describe the perception that many people hold of human service organizations of today?

The problems that arose in the senior's home in Gander could have been avoided if there had been a commitment to quality in customer services. A preoccupation with cost-cutting measures to the exclusion of consideration of quality led to an actual increase in costs. Had continuous quality improvement tools been used at this nursing home, managers and service workers alike would have recognized how important the "kitchen" was to the seniors and how depersonalized they felt when meals were being shipped in from outside the facility. They missed a feeling of home, the aromas of food being cooked, and the social interaction associated with the daily preparation and serving of meals. In short, the seniors felt they were being treated as commodities rather than as people or valued customers whose feelings and personal satisfaction were viewed as important.

NOW THE GOOD NEWS

A powerful new set of management tools exists that can address the many problems that human services organizations are facing today. This new set of tools is called total quality management (TQM). TQM is not just for administrators or management personnel. It is for service workers at all levels of the organization. It is important to note that individuals are called customers in the TQM vernacular and not clients or workers. Is this distinction important? Yes! All of us are customers in that we are both providers and recipients of service in the workplace. TQM practitioners hold to the view that customers have things "done for them," whereas clients (and workers) frequently have things "done to them." TQM is predicated on principles that may be viewed as part of an ethical foundation for the delivery of quality human services. Those principles include

- the importance of customer satisfaction with the services they receive
- the continuous quality improvement of customer services
- the evaluation of customer services
- a team approach to solving "quality" problems in service delivery.

It is only recently that these ideas have been systematized into a coherent set of tools that emphasize the continuous pursuit of quality. Although TQM leads toward greater effectiveness, it is not necessarily easy. At the heart of TQM is commitment to customer service and the gathering of facts to improve conditions to enhance customer satisfaction. TQM has embraced the adage that *without measurement and facts lasting improvements in quality are not possible.*

There are some who take a more cynical view of TQM and dismiss it as just another fad. Gummer and McCallion (1995) succinctly stated this dilemma by noting that "the management field is . . . fraught with uncertainties and insecurities . . . ; schemes for transforming organizational forms and practices come and go on a regular basis" (p. vii). Critics, in drawing attention to failures in quality initiatives, invoke the words "passing fad" to point to the problems that, they believe, will lead to TQM's ultimate decline. Brown, Hitchcock, and Willard (1994) present a powerful retort to these skeptics:

> We believe that this perspective is seriously flawed. After all, how can you dispute the need to delight customers and produce high quality services and products? As an organizational philosophy, total quality management is even more critical now than it was just 10 years ago. If there has been a failure, it is not one of philosophy: it is one of implementation. And if we allow management to go in search of a replacement, we only enable them to avoid facing their own failure, thus perpetuating the search for a silver bullet. (p. 5)

With the pressures of change coming from all sides in human services organizations, an approach to management is needed that is inclusive, dedicated to overcoming problems, and continuously improving the quality of services to customers. TQM addresses this need.

As previously noted, the gathering of information for decision making based on facts is essential to customer satisfaction in TQM. This process necessarily involves the use of statistical tools. Although statistics are often treated with some degree of wariness by human service practitioners, they need not be treated with fear. In fact, the reason for the use of statistical tools and other measurement methods in TQM is to present data in a clear, understandable, and effective manner while not compromising the accuracy of the information that is being presented. The collection and analysis of valid and useful information ultimately leads to TQM's focus on continuous quality improvement.

This book is intended to give the reader a first-hand experience in the use and application of a range of basic tools necessary to the development of an organizational culture of quality. The ultimate goal is to help practitioners to identify, solve, and evaluate quality problems in the workplace.

Perhaps it is appropriate to return to the question, "Why is this so important?" TQM is important to people everywhere—clients, workers, and administrators—because it promotes an organizational culture of quality that is focused not only on human service workers but also on the customers they serve. Why is a "culture of quality" necessary? A culture of quality is necessary so as to recapture the *service market* that has been devalued by an *economic market place* that puts primary value and interest on cost efficiencies and profits. The latter has moved us away from people and the needs of customers as the primary focus.

This all sounds good, but why do TQM programs fail? TQM programs fail because they are just that—programs. A successful TQM initiative promotes system-wide change intended to bring substantive transformation at all levels in the organization's culture.

The challenge posed by TQM in terms of change may be likened to the metamorphosis of a moth to a butterfly. It is no longer *business as usual*, if we are serious about coming to grips with the enormous challenges and changes that are occurring in human service delivery systems today. Berger (1994) analyzed four organizations that failed and then later went on to recapture their positions of strength. By noting the patterns that Berger put forth in her analysis we may learn important lessons. She notes,

> All four companies . . . were on top but couldn't stay there. They also shared the same basic reason for faltering. They were unable to successfully manage the process of great change demanded by the changes in their markets that resulted from changing customer requirements, shifts in competitor strategies or both.
>
> The troubled companies were either slow to discern the changes, or slow or reluctant to respond to them. Self-deception was a curse. The changes were regarded as passing fancies, or the companies perceived themselves as too big, too strong, or too good to worry about them . . . there was typically an inability to align key organization processes with the market, too many people who were satisfied with the status quo and opposed change . . . a lack of honest self-examination and a weak or detached involvement by the board of directors. (pp. 3–5)

Are you ready to change, to take a new approach both for yourself and for your customers? TQM challenges you to start the journey of quality. It is important to remember, however, that the journey does not have a final destination. Rather, its path is captured by the vision that change is indeed possible but involves an endless pursuit of quality and a commitment to continuous quality improvement.

The following chapters present the tools needed to succeed on this quality journey. Not only will you learn about the tools of TQM, but also you will be given the opportunity to experience and apply them. Still a little skeptical? Then read on. This is indeed a journey and we must let the journey begin!

REFERENCES

Brown, M. G., Hitchcock, D. E., & Willard, M. L. (1994). *Why TQM fails and what to do about it.* New York: Irwin Professional Publishing.

Berger, D. R. (1994). *The change management handbook.* New York: Irwin Professional Publishing.

Gummer, B., & McCallion, P. (Eds.). (1995). *Total quality management in the human services.* Albany, NY: Rockefeller College of Public Affairs and Policy.

2

Making TQM Work:
TQM and Quality Tools

TQM: ORIGINS AND CONCEPTS

TQM, a new management paradigm, has changed the corporate culture of many large organizations in this country and elsewhere, including IBM, Eastman Kodak, ITT, Xerox, American Express, Ford Motors, and Federal Express. The quality movement has been pioneered by three "gurus," Phillip B. Crosby, W. Edwards Deming, and Joseph M. Juran. Each of these theorists has enumerated several key tenets in his approach to quality management (see appendix A). What is so special about TQM that accounts for its popularity within many leading industrialized countries of the world, particularly the United States and Canada? Simply, the traditional approaches to management did not live up to expectations. Today's customers expect and demand products and services that meet their expectations in terms of quality. To remain competitive in this new climate, companies have had to face the challenge of quality head on and build it into their management systems. More than that, they had to change the corporate culture. It is no longer business as usual!

TQM was first introduced to North American companies through the work of W. Edwards Deming (Walton, 1986). He played a significant role after World War II in changing Japan from a second-rate, failing economy to a first-class, highly competitive industrial trading nation. Deming

(1986) saw the application of measurement tools and statistics in quality control as central to the success of quality management. Under his leadership, Japanese products became recognized around the world as being of the highest quality. Exports from Japan, traditionally viewed as relatively cheap and inferior, captured a significant segment of world markets because of the quality transformation that had taken place in that country.

Other quality management theorists, such as Phillip Crosby (1979) and Joseph Juran (1989), have played significant roles in articulating the central tenets of a quality approach to management and organizational development. Crosby saw the importance of "doing it right the first time" in an effort to promote the notion of *zero defects*, thus reducing the associated costs of having to make repairs or begin all over again. The theme of his approach underlined the importance of prevention of problems and defects through training, quality measurement, quality evaluation, and commitment to continuous improvement. Juran's work echoed somewhat similar themes in his emphasis on a structured approach to quality management that highlighted the three key processes of quality planning, quality control, and quality improvement (Juran, 1989, p. 24).

Although each of these early writers articulated particular tenets of TQM, they all shared a common concern: the consistent provision of quality products and services to meet customer needs. The central building blocks of effective quality management are seen as incorporating at least six key elements (Martin, 1993, p. 24):

1. Quality as a primary organizational goal;
2. Customers determine what quality is;
3. Customer satisfaction drives the organization;
4. Variation in processes must be understood and reduced;
5. Change is continuous and is accomplished by teams and teamwork;
6. Top management commitment to promoting a culture of quality, employee empowerment and a long-term perspective.

Gunther and Hawkins (1996) have incorporated each of these elements into their TQM model but have added other key process elements. These are quality education and training and statistical quality control, which give support to the development of an organizational culture of quality. Although organizations will vary in their approach to the introduction of TQM into their particular organization, most quality initiatives will incorporate most, if not all, of these key elements.

Probably the most consistent theme reflected in the implementation of TQM is the value placed on change and responsiveness to customer needs. It is this value that is viewed as such a necessary part of organizational life and culture within the TQM paradigm and that drives the commitment and quest for continuous quality improvement.

QUALITY MANAGEMENT AND HUMAN SERVICE ORGANIZATIONS

The quality revolution that has changed many facets of North America's corporate business community since the early 1980s has found its way into the corridors, offices, and board rooms of many nonprofit human service organizations. Within the past 5 years the quality management paradigm, commonly referred to as TQM, has been adopted by a wide range of public and private human service organizations across the United States and Canada. Recent examples are seen in postsecondary education (Bartley, 1996), children's residential and community services (Comstock & Price, 1996), acute and chronic health care facilities (Hassen, 1996; Henderson, 1996), publicly funded social services (Pollett, 1996; Henry, Wedel, & Czypinski, 1996), and rehabilitation services (Breen, Cazenave, & Dodge, 1996). Although this is not an exhaustive list, it is suggestive of the range of human service settings in which TQM has been successfully implemented. Empirical research on TQM in human service organizations has also begun. Boettcher (1995), using his TQM Index of Implementation (see appendix B), surveyed 41 human service organizations. Boettcher (1995) notes the following findings:

> In the 1995 study of human service organizations (n = 41) respondents were asked to estimate the extent to which their TQM programs have impacted on eight separate outcomes of service and/or employee behavior. The respondents reported substantial improvements in four service outcome categories including: client satisfaction (up in 66% of the agencies); frequency of client complaints (down in 5%); relations with funders (improved in 42%) and relations with community interest groups (improved in 36%). Substantial improvement was reported in employee morale (up in 51%); employee willingness to change (improved in 53%); and employee complaints (down in 38%). Employee absenteeism neither improved nor worsened under TQM. (p. 1)

It is not surprising that human service organizations find TQM to have a special attractiveness as a management system. Table 2.1 outlines several important tenets of social work and TQM. It is recognized

TABLE 2.1   Operational Tenets of Social Work and TQM

Social Work Tenets	Quality Tenets
Commitment to clients	Commitment to customers
Raise awareness of social costs of lack of services	Raise awareness about cost of non-quality in services
Raise awareness of client needs	Raise quality awareness regarding customer needs
Take corrective action to solve psychosocial problems	Take corrective action to solve quality problem (potential for change)
Empower clients	Empower customers
Build support groups	Establish quality-oriented work teams
Act on valid information	Make decisions based on facts
Evaluate programs	Measure for continuous quality
Build self-confidence	Drive out fear
Identify causes of problem	Identify barriers to quality
Promote skills development	Promote quality learning through education and training
Establish goals with clients	Establish quality goals with customers (internal, external, and ultimate)
Recognize strengths	Recognize performance
Life-long learning	Continuous quality improvement
Build quality of life	Build quality organizational culture

that the philosophy and values of this management paradigm are congruent with major tenets underlying other humanistic professions, such as medicine, nursing, teaching, and pastoral counseling. Belief in the dignity of the person is not dissimilar to TQM's commitment to and concern for customers and their changing needs. The notion of continuous quality improvement complements the belief that people have the potential to change and develop their skills and capacities to meet new challenges and opportunities. This is a central tenet underlying all intervention methodologies involving human relations technology. Teamwork and customer empowerment both have particular meaning to human service professionals. They place high value on cooperation and support in human relations and decision making. Associated with this is their concern for individuals and groups who lack the necessary resources to enjoy an adequate standard of living. The relationship between this concern and the commitment to service and product quality is clear. Both are supportive of the notion that people are important and that quality can and will be personally defined and operationalized in human relationships at all levels, both in the community and in the workplace.

For many people, TQM does present somewhat of a paradox in that its appeal appears to transcend organizational boundaries that have traditionally been viewed as different and distinct. Commonalities between the corporate sector, concerned with profit, and the not-for-profit human service sector may appear as quite anomalous to some. Nevertheless, it is these commonalities, coupled with the failure of many traditional management approaches to solve our current problems, that have led many business and human service organizations to adopt TQM. Developing an organizational culture of quality is quite distinct and different from maintaining a culture of productivity characteristic of traditional management. Gunther and Hawkins (1996) have noted these differences (Table 2.2).

A culture of quality is one that is responsive and adaptive to new and changing circumstances. It places a high value on process monitoring in the interest of quality improvements, rather than a preoccupation with outcomes, as in a culture of productivity. It promotes a collectivist orientation in which teamwork and cooperation are operationalized in a more horizontal, decentralized organizational structure. It is interesting to note the predictions that Skidmore (1983) posed more than 15 years ago regarding what social work administration would be like around the year 2000. He predicted the following:

1. Developing theoretical frameworks in social work administration
2. Forecasting and social services
3. More focus on accountability in the delivery of social services
4. Delivery of social services
5. Improved staff development programs
6. More use of community processes
7. Improved public relations
8. More effective committees in operation
9. Improved supervision
10. Emphasis on leadership in social work.
11. Shifts in budgeting
12. More effective communication
13. Increased interest in feelings of staff
14. Development of participatory management
15. Increase in research

Skidmore's predictions (1983, pp. 248–254) point to key changes in organizational processes, many of which have been profiled in the TQM paradigm. These include teamwork, staff development and training programs, use of quality improvement teams, improved communication

TABLE 2.2   Characteristics of the Organizational Cultures of Quality and Productivity

Culture of Quality	Culture of Productivity
Focus on quality	Focus on productivity
Customer focus	Market focus
Horizontal organizational structures that are integrated and aligned	Vertical organizational structures that are segmented and centralized
Process monitoring	Outcome monitoring
Statistically based decision making	Vertical and rational sequences of decision making
Creative thinking	Regimented thinking
Continuous quality improvement	Outcome-results-oriented management
Top management participation, commitment, and action	Top management support for operations
Collective orientation	Individual orientation
Teamwork performance	Individual performance
Innovation (individual/organization)	Organizational conformity
Change process	Change individual

Adapted from *Total Quality Management in Human Service Organizations* (p. 15), by J. Gunther and F. Hawkins (Eds.), 1996, New York: Springer Publishing Co.

with internal and external customers, and enhanced accountability through fact-based decision making and research.

TQM is not a quick fix to the problems facing human service organizations today. Rather, it is viewed as a long-term process of continuous change in which the emphasis is on partnerships with customers and a commitment to learning new ways to improve quality (Gunther & Hawkins, 1996). Within the current climate of heightened sensitivity to public expenditures; scarce dollars; and rapid social, economic, and political change, organizations require management systems that are adaptive to change and able to demonstrate the efficient and effective use of scarce resources. TQM not only incorporates a belief system that sees change as natural and inevitable, but also presents a variety of tools to assist in the challenge of continuous quality improvement and organizational accountability.

Quality in organizations does not evolve naturally and requires more than wishful thinking. TQM demands the production of information and data related to products and service to guide effective decision making and continuous improvement. Management on the basis of fact moves employees away from an intuitive approach, to a management mode in which the collection of accurate information is intrinsic in day-to-day activities at all levels. The implementation of effective quality tools and management measurement systems serves to assist employees in clarifying organizational goals and objectives within the context of quality planning. It provides the means whereby processes and outcomes are monitored and changes are made in the interest of quality improvement.

TQM's central and most important tenet is commitment to customer service. This is the starting point for all TQM initiatives if they are to be successful. All activities must be grounded on this fundamental principle to ensure a sense of purpose and direction. Such a commitment cannot be taken for granted, however. Organizational readiness to implement a quality initiative must begin with the assessment of an organization's readiness. This is the first and most important step and involves the question "Is this organization ready for a TQM initiative?" The Gunther and Hawkins TQM model articulates the various steps and activities involved in the implementation of quality management within a human services context (see appendix C). Each phase of the model involves the use of quality tools to determine the status, nature, and character of organizational variables relevant in the ultimate realization of quality products and services.

TQM TOOLS

TQM tools are used to obtain valid and useful information in the day to day operations of human service organizations. Such information is essential to decision making for quality improvements. A frequent complaint from managers is difficulty in finding time to train staff in the tools of quality. It is not that this process is viewed as unimportant. The implementation of training programs is critically important to the successful development and maintenance of a quality service delivery system. The pressures of time constraints and limited resources are real issues in today's workplace. For this reason care has been taken in the selection and organization of material for this handbook. The application and use of quality tools are grounded in real life situations that occur daily in human service organizations. Measurement tools are presented in a manner that addresses important questions related to quality and the promotion of constructive change. The skills involved in measurement are presented in simple language so that they make sense and can be easily related to common workplace activities. For some people, measurement, evaluation, and research carry an aura of mystery and generate feelings of insecurity because these processes are associated with the notion of complicated statistical procedures.

Although this may be true for some types of study and research, it is not true for most quality measurement tools. This handbook sets out to demystify measurement and the use of measurement tools so that they can be understood and used within the context of solving day-to-day work problems. Continuous quality improvement challenges human services professionals to be at their best and, equally important, to appreciate that such initiatives can indeed make a difference in our organizations and our communities.

Within TQM, services are challenged to stand the test of real accountability. They must be measured against standards and expectations of customers, whether they be frontline workers, community funders, clients, or others. Indeed, the needs and aspirations of customers must remain primary. A word of caution is in order, however. The rapid pace of change in today's world makes any assumptions held about customers and their needs somewhat tenuous. The mobility and diversity of today's population make it imperative that human service organizations become aware and responsive to the changing needs of customers and develop as true learning organizations. Senge (1990) describes learning organizations as the only ones that will truly excel in the future because they "discover how to tap people's commitment and capacity to learn at all levels" (p. 4). Routine and systematic service monitoring provides valuable information in the creation and promotion of a quality learning environment and culture of quality.

Measurement tools provide human service organizations with the means to exercise professional judgment as to what works and what does not work. It enables the analysis of work processes so that data sets become the vehicles whereby workers learn from current and past experiences. The continuous quality improvement cycle promotes not only a spirit of ownership of organizational problems but also a spirit of achievement in the pursuit of quality solutions. Such a spirit captures the essence of TQM, the continuous pursuit of quality being a journey, rather than a destination. Measurement tools give meaning to that journey by providing direction and purpose. Yogi Berra stated it most succinctly "You have to be very careful if you don't know where you are going, you might not get there" (MacDorman, MacDorman, & Fleming, 1995, p. 13). Measurement tools can serve to guide human service professionals in their continuing quest for quality.

Qualitative versus Quantitative Quality Tools

Although quantitative measurement tools hold a place in TQM, it should be noted that organizational statistics must be interpreted. TQM and quality are dynamic, with their primary purpose being the self-actualization of consumers. Quantitative tools can serve this purpose. On the other hand, qualitative tools draw attention to a different dimension of the management of quality. Although quantitative tools give an aura of precision, they are frequently viewed as being static. Qualitative tools, however, are viewed as being more dynamic in their ability to help conceptualize a problem, add greater depth of understanding, and bring a participating consciousness to quality problems.

Dabbs (1982) attempts to draw a distinction between qualitative and quantitative approaches. He notes,

> *Quality* is essential to the nature of things. On the other hand, *quantity* is elementally an amount of something. *Quality* refers to the what, how, when, and where of a thing -its essence and ambience. Qualitative research thus refers to the meanings, concepts, definitions, characteristics, metaphors, symbols, and descriptions of things. In contrast, *quantitative research* refers to counts and measures of things. (p. 2)

Although this book does not advocate a qualitative approach over a quantitative approach in TQM measurement, it does see merit in combining these approaches. Quality tools and measurement do not exist in a vacuum. Both are essential to a culture of quality.

A final word about the use of quality tools in human services merits attention. Human service professionals face special challenges as they face the new world of the 21st century with its cyberspace communication and instant access to information. Measurement tools provide the means whereby the realities of the workplace can be communicated to others in ways that were not thought possible a few short years ago. In today's world of rapid and inexpensive electronic communication, professionals have the opportunity to learn from the experiences of others, both locally and globally. Benchmarking (Galea-Curmi & Hawkins, 1996) can have special meaning within this context, because information can be shared so rapidly. Professionals can learn from the best practices of other colleagues and delivery systems around the world. Partnerships with human service organizations in other countries have the potential to build a culture of organizational learning that is truly global.

REFERENCES

Bartley, M. (1996). Total quality management in higher education. In J. Gunther & F. Hawkins (Eds.), *Total quality management in human service organizations.* New York: Springer Publishing Co.

Berg, B. L. (1989). *Qualitative research methods.* Needham Heights, MA: Allyn and Bacon.

Boettcher, R. (1995). *Study of the application of the TQM index to human service organizations.* Columbus, OH: The Ohio State University.

Breen, S., Cazenave, L., Dodge, B., Kliebart, K., & Moore, P. (1996). *Total quality management in human service organizations.* New York: Springer Publishing Co.

Comstock, C., & Price, S. (1996). Hillside Children's Center. In J. Gunther & F. Hawkins (Eds.), *Total quality management in human service organizations.* New York: Springer Publishing Co.

Crosby, P. B. (1979). *Quality is free: The art of making quality certain.* New York: McGraw-Hill.

Dabbs, J. M. (1982). Making things visible. In J. Van Maanen (Ed.), *Varieties of qualitative research.* Beverly Hills, CA: Sage.

Deming, W. E. (1986). *Out of the crisis.* Cambridge, MA: Massachusetts Institute of Technology, Center for Advanced Engineering Study.

Galea-Curmi, E., & Hawkins, F. (1996). Benchmarking. In J. Gunther & F. Hawkins (Eds.), *Total quality management in human service organizations.* New York: Springer Publishing Co.

Gunther, J., & Hawkins, F. (Eds.). (1996). *Total quality management in human service organizations.* New York: Springer Publishing Co.

Hassen, P. (1996). The St. Joseph's Health Centre story. In J. Gunther & F. Hawkins (Eds.), *Total quality management in human service organizations.* New York: Springer Publishing Co.

Henderson, P. (1996). Freeport Hospital Health Care Village. In J. Gunther & F. Hawkins (Eds.), *Total quality management in human service organizations.* New York: Springer Publishing Co.

Henry, G., Wedel, K., & Czypinski, K. (1996). Quality Oklahoma and the Oklahoma Department of human services. In J. Gunther & F. Hawkins (Eds.), *Total quality management in human services.* New York: Springer Publishing Co.

Juran, J. M. (1989). *Juran on leadership for quality: An executive handbook.* New York: Free Press.

Martin, L. L. (1993). *Total quality management in human service organizations.* Newbury Park, CA: Sage.

MacDorman, L. C., MacDorman, J. C., & Fleming, W. T. (1995). *The quality journey: A TQM roadmap for public transportation.* Washington, DC: National Academy Press.

Pollet, K. (1996). Total quality management within the Newfoundland and Labrador Department of Social Services. In J. Gunther & F. Hawkins (Eds.), *Total quality management in human service organizations.* New York: Springer Publishing Co.

Senge, P. M. (1990). *The fifth discipline: The art and practice of the learning organization.* New York: Currency Doubleday.

Skidmore, R. A. (1983). *Social work administration: Dynamic management and human relationships.* Englewood Cliffs, NJ: Prentice Hall.

Walton, M. (1986). *The Deming management method.* New York: Putnam.

Training: Tools in Planning for Continuous Quality Improvement

Training is an essential part of both initiating and maintaining a quality of culture. The ultimate goal of training is the institutionalization of TQM. The success of any quality initiative will depend quite fundamentally on the attention and resources that are committed to the ongoing training and development of staff members. Gunther and Hawkins (1996), in addressing the need for quality training and education, place this within the context of organizational change and the development of a culture of quality. They state, "The undertaking of a TQM initiative is a complex task fostering many changes within an organization's culture. As a consequence of moving toward a culture of quality, training and education are necessary to help in the management of change" (p. 29).

This chapter will examine the various dimensions of training from the perspective of organizational change, with explanation as to why this is so important to the success of TQM. Some attention will be given to the planning and implementation of training from the perspective of several key questions that need to be addressed. Several quality-oriented training tools will be described and applied in a case example involving a human service organization in the health care sector. The following section will focus on three areas of concern in the need to make training part of the organization's culture. The concluding section will provide an experiential exercise so that the quality tools of training used in TQM can be mastered.

THE IMPORTANCE OF TRAINING WITHIN TQM

It is acknowledged by most professionals today that the pace of social, economic, and technological change is so rapid that keeping on top of one's job is proving to be a major challenge. Skidmore (1995) states, "We live in a world in which knowledge is being added at a geometric rate. . . . In fact, so many publications are available today that no one worker can begin to read all the current literature about social work and its services" (p. 269). The current information explosion makes it imperative that programs of training be provided to ensure that professionals remain on the cutting edge of developments in their respective fields. Within the context of TQM, such programs of training are viewed as intrinsic to the organization's mission and commitment to provide valued quality service to its customer.

A second and related facet of the need for training within the TQM paradigm is recognition that customer needs are not static. Rather, they are constantly changing and being shaped by a range of variables that are often difficult to predict. Training within TQM is viewed as being both proactive and reactive. Effective quality management involves the training of all staff in the basic philosophy and skills of TQM. In this sense training initiatives will be proactive in ensuring that all staff receive a basic level of training. On the other hand, human service organizations are unique, and each organization will have special needs and circumstances that will have to be addressed in the design and implementation of training. This is another way of saying that training will serve the unique needs of internal and external customers.

Training programs will vary from organization to organization, but some of the more common objectives are outlined below:

- To introduce the basic philosophy and tenets of TQM
- To develop strategic quality planning initiatives
- To assess an organization's readiness to commence a TQM initiative

- To develop a quality mission and vision statement for the organization
- To develop understanding and skills related to team development
- To develop understanding and skills related to the use of measurement tools
- To assess the efficiency of work processes so that the continuous quality improvement cycle is constantly emphasized
- To develop skills related to problem solving and consensus building
- To develop an understanding of the nature of organizational culture, the operational values and norms influencing decision making in the current culture and strategies to promote a culture of quality
- To promote an awareness of the need for an active learning organization and develop strategies to enhance quality learning
- To strengthen a sense of partnership with key customers and stakeholders in a shared commitment to provide quality service
- To promote the implementation of problem solving strategies through the development of project teams

MODELS OF TRAINING WITHIN TQM

Two basic approaches to training are documented in the literature. The first may be described as an *employee development model* with a philosophy of implementing training in a *cascading strategy,* beginning with management personnel at the top of the organization. Following their exposure to training, key managers will in turn train other staff members, either working on their team or within a particular functional area of the organization. Middle managers will assume the responsibility for training those below them, and so on down to the frontline staff.

The second approach may be described as *the expert trainer model.* This model uses an expert in TQM who trains the staff in various sectors of the organization. The expert trainer may be a staff member or someone external to the organization who is brought in as a consultant and trainer to promote the TQM initiative. These models may be viewed as representing two ideal types, since most organizations will use variants of both training models. For example, the case studies presented in Gunther and Hawkins (1996) illustrate the range of possibilities. "Quality Oklahoma" describes training initiatives that began outside the organization, with TQM specialists providing training to internal staff training specialists. These training experts, in turn, implemented a training program that began at the top of the organization and in a cascading approach moved down the organization until employees at all levels were exposed to training (Henry, Wedel, & Czypinski, 1996, pp. 90–92).

"The St. Joseph's Health Centre Story" describes a TQM initiative that began with the adaptation of "industrial" model training materials to health care, followed by the employment of an in-house director of TQM (Hassen, 1996, pp. 56–58). This *inside expert* assumed a training role that involved a train-the-trainer approach for other sectors of the organization. One can see that the approaches to training will vary, depending on the needs and resources of the organization; however, the basic thrust of all training is to continually develop an organizational infrastructure to meet customer needs.

TQM TRAINING PROGRAMS

To achieve quality results in the development of training programs one must have a clear sense of purpose and direction. This is only possible within a program framework that identifies the objectives to be achieved through various training initiatives. Earlier in this chapter, we identified a number of possible training objectives. To illustrate the implementation of training and the application of specific tools it will be useful to examine the case of the Hemingway Cancer Treatment Centre (HCTC). Particular attention will be given to the use of two tools: Plan-Do-Check-Act (PDCA) and force field analysis.

The first tool, force field analysis, is a process analysis tool that facilitates the identification and understanding of the various forces (variables) that operate in a particular situation. It was first introduced by Kurt Lewin (1954) as a systematic approach to understanding organizations and the forces that operate to maintain the status quo and those that push for change. He suggested that in any force field there were "driving forces" that promoted change and "restraining forces" that resisted change. Kanji and Asher (1996) have suggested a seven-step procedure for implementing force field analysis. They note,

1. Identify the current situation. This is likely to reflect the problem statement. Place this statement in the center at the top of the page. Below the statement draw a vertical line to the bottom of the page.
2. Identify where you should be: the desired state. This is placed on the right-hand side of the page at the top. Again, draw a vertical line to the bottom. The aim is to move the center line to the right-hand side, moving from the current situation to where you want to be.
3. Brainstorm all the driving forces: these forces move the line to the right (positive forces).

4. Brainstorm all the forces that hinder: these forces move the line to the left (negative forces).
5. Estimate the ease of increasing helping forces, using a scale of 1–5 as follows: 5, very easy; 4, easy; 3, medium; 2, difficult; 1, very difficult.
6. Estimate the impact of hindering forces, again using a scale of 1–5 as follows: 5, very easy; 4, easy; 3, medium; 2, difficult; 1, very difficult.
7. Work out the priority number of each force by multiplying (5) by (6). (p. 98)

The second tool, PDCA, often referred to as the Shewhart/Deming cycle (Saylor, 1992, p. 55), has both process control and process improvement features. Process control is designed to prevent problems from happening, whereas process improvement refers to activities designed to enhance product or service quality. The usefulness and application of this tool will be seen in relation to building a quality training program.

Conway (1993) illustrates the fundamental processes inherent in the PDCA cycle (see Figure 3.1). Although Tague (1995) explicates the steps necessary to implement the PDCA cycle, she notes that the implementation procedures for the Plan-Do-Check-Act cycle are as follows:

1. Plan: Recognize an opportunity and plan the change.
2. Do: Test the change, carry out a small scale study.
3. Check: Review the test, analyse the results, and identify learnings.
4. Act: Take action based on what you learned in the check step. If you were successful, incorporate the learnings from the test into wider changes. If the change did not work, go through the cycle again with a different plan. (pp. 218–219)

Before proceeding to the application of these tools, a brief description of the Hemingway Cancer Treatment Centre is provided.

CASE: THE HEMINGWAY CANCER TREATMENT CENTRE

The HCTC was established to serve the needs of citizens in a primarily rural area. The Centre is located in a capital city (population 150,000) and serves a population of approximately 500,000 people. Services are provided on an outpatient basis. In addition to the services provided at the Centre's main facility in the city, a decentralized model of service delivery is in place, with four rural district clinics serving citizens in more distant areas. Services are provided by a multidisciplinary health care team consisting of medical oncologists, radiologists, nurses, social workers, and other paraprofes-

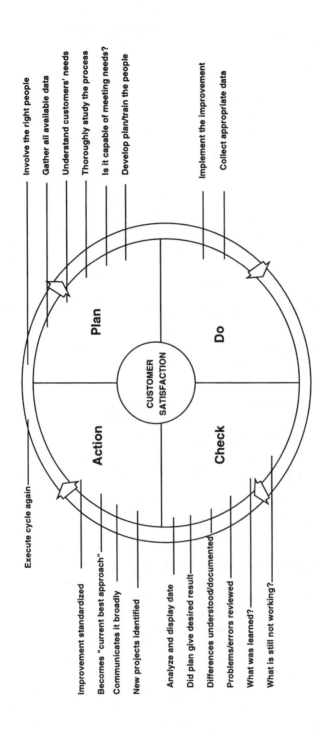

FIGURE 3.1 The P-D-C-A cycle.

sionals and clinical support staff. The HCTC is administered by a chief executive order (CEO) and a medical director, both of whom report to the Centre's 12-person board of directors.

Since its opening in 1992, the HCTC has received strong financial support from the government and the general public through tax dollars and annual public appeals. In the last 2 years, health care funding from the government has been reduced in all areas as part of a general push to reduce the public debt, eliminate deficit financing of public programs, and balance the budget. The HCTC has been caught in this squeeze and is facing two challenges: (1) How to reduce costs while maintaining an acceptable level of quality services and (2) how to prepare for a successful accreditation review within the next 2 years. To address these challenges, the executive group, with the assistance and support of the board of directors, has established a quality council to foster the development of a quality culture within HCTC through the implementation of TQM. It was believed that the problems associated with cost cutting could best be addressed within this paradigm. The concern for more efficient use of resources needed to be balanced with a concern for building an effective quality organization and a continuous quality improvement (CQI) cycle.

The Hemingway Quality Council (HQC) consists of eight members representing the major functional areas of the organization, including administration, medicine, nursing, consumers, and the general public. The chair of the HQC is a member of HCTC's board of directors and reports directly to them.

Application of Force Field Analysis

The first meetings of the HQC provided members with an opportunity to discuss various facets of the center's work and activities, recognizing that there was a fairly high level of commitment and understanding regarding the major tenets of TQM and how it could be operationalized. It was decided to invite tenders from several local area consultants to assist in the initial assessment of the organization's readiness and needs preparatory to a full-scale implementation of TQM.

A review of the proposals and their associated costs with a range of possible outcomes led the group to the conclusion that much of the information to be provided in such an assessment was already known. It was decided to move directly into a program of TQM training for all staff. A group meeting was called by the CEO, and a brief overview and background were given regarding the board's decision to move forward with the implementation of TQM training. This was placed within the context of budget cutbacks, the need for efficiency, and the upcoming accreditation review 2 years hence.

Force field analysis was presented as a diagnostic tool to identify and understand some of the factors operating in the center to both help and hinder the success of this quality initiative. Participants were given a force field analysis inventory to identify the *driving forces* and the *restraining forces* relevant to the current situation and the need for change. The participants broke into small groups and, following a discussion of the results from the individual inventories, were asked to construct a force field naming the most critical factors. The relative strength of each factor was given a weighting from 1 to 5 (1, very low; 5, very high). The results of the small group meeting were shared with the larger group and used as a basis for discussion on how to best proceed. Table 3.1 presents the findings of the force field analysis developed from the group meeting.

TABLE 3.1 Findings of the Force Field Analysis for HCTC's Quality Initiative: Strength of Factors Promoting/Hindering Success

Driving forces	Strength	→	←	Strength	Restraining forces
Staff commitment to quality	5	→	←	3	Too little time to implement
Pride in the organization	5	→	←	2	Professional autonomy
Challenge of accreditation	3	→	←	5	Lack of vision and a plan
Push for efficiencies	2	→	←	5	Lack of skills/tools
Recognition of the need for improvements	2	→	←	2	Fear of losing jobs

From a brain storming of the information in Table 3.1 related to the driving and restraining forces, a prioritization of the *ease of changing* these forces was established and an assessment of their *impact* was determined. A training program with the following training objectives were identified and presented to the board of directors:

1. To train all staff members in the basic concepts of TQM and develop a quality vision statement for the organization within 6 months.

2. To train all management staff in the basic measurement tools of TQM within 6 months.
3. To develop a series of focus groups with representatives from all sectors of the organization to identify areas of concern and explore strategies for quality improvement within the next 12 months.
4. To identify and implement at least four quality improvement projects linked with specific performance measures and outcome indicators within the next 12 months.

PDCA Implementation

The HQC decided to contract with an outside consultant to achieve objectives 1 and 2. It was believed that objectives 3 and 4 could be achieved through the training initiatives of key managers in working with their staff. Four months after the decision to proceed with this quality initiative it was decided to introduce the first quality improvement project, a project to reduce the waiting times for patients with appointments at the clinic. It was decided to implement the PDCA quality improvement tool as a means of monitoring the problem as well as a vehicle for building strategies to improve the situation. Decisions were made in consultation with representatives from each of the internal customer groups (i.e., doctors, nurses, technicians, social workers, patients, and support staff) and represented the various phases of the problem-solving cycle (PDCA).

The PDCA tool was chosen as the primary implementation method to begin the quality initiative, with the goal of institutionalizing TQM into the agency's work processes. The first quality improvement project addressed the problem of waiting times for patients at HCTC. With this priority in place the following PDCA processes evolved.

Step 1—Plan   FORM A PROJECT TEAM.
- Describe the current process and identify current service providers in this process.
- Identify potential causes of the problem.
- Identify actions to address the problem and relevant process measures.
PLAN THE CHANGE WITH DESIRED SERVICE OUTCOMES.

Step 2—Do   • Consult current service providers regarding
                   current process and, if necessary, modify the
                   plan (return to step 1).
                 • IMPLEMENT THE CHANGE PLAN (agreed on in
                   step 1).
                 • Collect process data.
Step 3—Check   • ANALYZE FINDINGS AND DRAW CONCLUSIONS.
                 • Analyze data and continue actions.
                 • Decide to change actions based on data find-
                   ings.
Step 4—Act   • CONTINUE PLAN or make REVISIONS (based
                   on data).
                 • Go to step 1 (to maintain gains) or
                 • Begin the PDCA cycle again.

The project team charged with the responsibility of addressing
the problem found that patient waiting times could be reduced by
introducing the following changes:

1. Have patients complete various forms prior to attendance at the
   clinic.
2. Monitor patient movement through the clinic and allow patients
   to skip steps if there is a delay.
3. Have physicians assign delay codes (to unexpected contingencies)
   so that nurses can estimate *arrival time* of physicians, giving patient
   freedom to make alternate plans, rather than simply having to wait.
4. Give appointment managers flexibility in cuing patients, so that
   special circumstances can be accommodated.
5. Initiate regular *monthly reviews* of the factors playing into physical
   delays, with strategies put in place to minimize problems (implement PDCA to review and monitor the success of plan).
6. Take greater care in the setting realistic appointment times.

After 1 year the patient waiting times were reduced by 40%.

CONCLUSION

Training plays an important part in the implementation of all facets of
TQM. Without ongoing learning and training there is no CQI. The HCTC
case illustrates the use of two quality tools in the initiation of training.
The first tool, force field analysis, is a valuable assessment and learning

tool and can be used to enhance understanding of the factors operating in the work environment to promote or impede change. The second tool, PDCA, can be used in all phases of process improvement. It provides participants with a framework from which to plan and implement quality initiatives. Essentially, it is a problem-solving tool that reflects the qualities of a true *open system* in which changes in the workplace, relevant to the problem at hand, are quickly incorporated in the strategies devised to bring about change.

EXPERIENTIAL EXERCISE: QUALITY TRAINING

Force Field Analysis

The following exercise can be helpful in identifying and understanding the nature of factors or forces that are operational in the current work environment to either promote change or maintain the status quo. The goal of the exercise is to identify the forces that promote change and those that prevent change.

To begin, divide into small groups (three to five people). The members of each group should identify something that they would like to change in a human service organization. On a flip chart identify the driving forces that push for change and the restraining forces that support the status quo. Now, estimate the strength of the helping forces and the strength of the hindering forces on a scale of 1 to 5 as follows: 5, very high; 4, high; 3, moderate; 2, low; 1, very low. Discuss possible strategies to increase (or decrease) the strength of specific forces. Discuss the findings with the larger group. Record your responses below.

_____
_____
_____
_____
_____
_____
_____
_____
_____
_____
_____
_____
_____

_____
_____
_____
_____
_____
_____
_____
_____

As a variation to this exercise have your group identify a quality problem of common concern and carry out the following activities:

- Have each participant in turn describe what he or she understands to be the problem.
- Have each participant identify what he or she considers to be the most important factor causing the current problem.
- Give each person an opportunity to identify the key customers in the current problem and explain why this person is a customer.
- Select one aspect of the current problem that participants would like to change and decide which factors are the easiest to change and which are the most difficult. State your reasons below for your choice of facts.

_____
_____
_____
_____
_____
_____
_____
_____
_____
_____
_____
_____
_____
_____
_____
_____
_____
_____

The PDCA Cycle

The following exercise is intended to deepen the reader's skill and understanding of the value of the PDCA tool and to promote creative thinking regarding its application to quality problems within a human service organization. The goal of the exercise is to increase understanding of the various components of the PDCA cycle and explore process areas in human service organizations where it can be applied. Before initiating the experiential exercise it is important to review the concepts and readings in this chapter on the PDCA cycle. When this is completed, divide into groups of four people and assign a letter corresponding to each of the four letters of this quality tool to each participant. Ask each member to write down on paper what actions they think are involved in the quality improvement phase (represented by the letter each has been assigned) of the PDCA cycle. Smaller groups may then report to the larger group, comparing and discussing the variations in the responses, posting the findings on flip charts. Record the findings in the space below.

_____

_____

_____

_____

_____

_____

_____

_____

_____

_____

_____

_____

_____

_____

_____

_____

_____

_____

_____

_____

_____

When you are finished presenting your PDCA findings, answer the following questions individually and then discuss the findings with the group. Record your discussion below.

- Is the PDCA tool applicable to individual problems?
- Describe the problem-solving approach adopted by a human service organization with which you are familiar?
- What is the most difficult step in the PDCA cycle? Explain.
- What measures are in place to determine success in your current place of employment (or association)? Do you think they are valid?
- Explain why the PDCA cycle can be described as a learning tool.

Write your answers to the questions here.

_____
_____
_____
_____
_____
_____
_____
_____
_____
_____
_____
_____
_____
_____
_____
_____
_____
_____
_____
_____
_____
_____
_____
_____
_____
_____

REFERENCES

Conway, E. C. (1993). Total quality: An integrating concept. In W. F. Christopher & C. G. Thor (Eds.), *Handbook for productivity measurement and improvement*. Portland, OR: Productivity Press.

Gunther, J., & Hawkins, F. (1996). *Total quality management in human service organizations*. New York: Springer Publishing Co.

Hassen, P. (1996). The St. Josephs Health Centre Story. In J. Gunther & F. Hawkins (Eds.), *Total quality management in human service organizations*. New York: Springer Publishing Co.

Henry, G., Wedel, K., & Czypinski, K. (1996). Quality Oklahoma and the Oklahoma Department of Human Services. In J. Gunther & F. Hawkins (Eds.), *Total quality management in human services*. New York: Springer Publishing Co.

Kanji, G. K., & Asher, M. (1996). *100 methods for total quality management*. Thousand Oaks, CA: Sage.

Lewin, K. (1954). Group decision and social change. In E. Maccoby & T. Newcomb (Eds.), *Readings in social psychology*. New York: Holt, Rinehart & Winston.

Saylor, J. H. (1992). *TQM field manual*. New York: McGraw-Hill.

Skidmore, R. A. (1995). *Social work administration: Dynamic management and human relationships*. Needham Heights, MA: Allyn and Bacon.

Tague, N. R. (1995). *The quality toolbox*. Milwaukee, WI: ASQC, Quality Press.

Team Building:
TQM Development
and Employee
Empowerment Tools

Gunther and Hawkins (1996) have noted that teams are essential to the success of any TQM initiative. They stress,

> The ultimate purpose of a team is to improve customer satisfaction via the quality process. The Oxford Dictionary defines a team as "a set of persons working together . . . displaying a willingness to act for group rather than individual effort." Effort means quality teamwork directed toward the HSO as a whole, rather than toward specific functional areas. (p. 40)

Although the importance of developing effective work teams should be obvious, there are many managers in human service organizations who overlook this area. Perhaps this is because many managers do not understand how to develop a team culture that produces continuous quality improvement (CQI) and a high level of performance. Because they are beyond the scope of the individual, the quality and performance challenges that human service organizations confront today must be addressed by teams. The synergy created by teams leads to enhanced performance. Teams will outperform individuals acting alone or in larger organizational groupings, especially when performance requires multiple skills, judgments, and experiences, as Katzenbach and Smith have noted (1993, p. 9).

In order to develop a team-oriented culture, certain assumptions must be factored into the development of the initial team culture. Schaaf and Kaeter (1992) stress

> One key to building a true quality culture is building commitment from all corners of the organization—not only among managers, where power has traditionally resided, but even more importantly among those who for many years have been systematically disenfranchised. People unaccustomed to acting in empowered ways need a little time to get the hang of it. And their fragile sense of involvement will be quickly broken if they are constantly overridden by management fiat or vocal clique. (p. 104)

Most of all, it should be remembered that building a collective team-oriented culture that stresses continuous improvement takes time. The alternative to time and patience is service that is strictly anchored to productivity and not customer satisfaction. The case of Acme hospital presented in this chapter is an example of how to develop quality teams.

CASE: THE ACME HOSPITAL

The Acme hospital has long served the needs of chronically ill mental health patients in the state of Minorka. Hospital services are centralized and organized according to functional areas. Typically, patients have been served as long-term residents of the institution. A recent court action has ordered the hospital to release patients to the "least restrictive environment" available, however. In order to respond to the court order, the Acme hospital has decided to develop a TQM initiative to achieve the quality outcomes associated with the court order. The most immediate task is to develop a self-directed team and put in place the associated work processes necessary to achieve the broad parameters of the court mandated objective.

TRANSITION TEAM BUILDING

Intrinsic to addressing the Acme Hospital case is the central notion of team development. Prior to entering any team building initiative the concept of a *team* must be differentiated from the concept of a *group*. Essentially, a team is a group of people who must coordinate their activities to achieve a team-defined goal. On the other hand, a group is two or more persons who are assembled and have some unifying attribute (e.g., social workers, psychologists, etc.). Shonk (1982) stressed this point by noting "the common goal or task and the coordination required determines whether a team exists" (p. 2). Shonk developed a tool that has heuristic implications in the advancement of any quality-oriented team development. He proposed a set of questions to discern whether a group should function as a team. Shonk stated that before developing a team-building initiative, a group assessment should be made along the dimensions of goals, interdependence, collaboration, and time frame. Table 4.1 presents Shonk's critical questions and notes that "the higher the interdependence of the team, the higher the need for team work" (p. 5). Within the context of the table this would be seen in a greater frequency of A rather than B responses.

CONSENSUS MODEL

By using Shonk's questions, the Acme Hospital determined that a team-building initiative was necessary. Once this decision was made, the hospital decided to organize teams according to geographic units. Teams in the hospital then decided to use the quality tool of consensus in order to bring shared knowledge and understanding to their work processes. Consensus is a convergent process whereby teams agree on a further course of action in the CQI cycle. Consensus is reached by a team when

- team members have actively participated in decision or task analysis processes
- a decision has been reached that all team members are willing to live with and support

Implementation of the Consensus Model

The model for reaching consensus in the quality paradigm contains the following steps:

TABLE 4.1   Critical Questions Involved in Team Building

The following questions will help you examine to what extent your group is interdependent and, therefore, to what extent it needs to function as a team. Circle the letter for the statement (A or B) that best describes your group or team.

I.   GOALS
     A. Members have common goals or tasks that require working to-
        gether.
     B. The goals and tasks of members are separate.

II. INTERDEPENDENCE
     A. Actions or decisions of any one member impact upon the work
        of the other members.
     B. Members can make decisions or take actions without impacting
        upon the work of other members.

III. COLLABORATION
     A. Work can be accomplished most effectively by members working
        together.
     B. Work can best be accomplished by members working alone.

IV. TIME FRAME
     A. Activities must be coordinated on a daily/weekly basis.
     B. Members can work for long periods of time, weeks/months, with-
        out coordinating activities with one another.

From *Working in teams: A practical manual for improving work groups* (pp. 5–7), by J. H. Shonk, 1982, New York: AMACOM.

1. In problem definition the problem is stated in terms of internal and external customer needs.
2. Several alternatives to the problem are generated through the use of brain storming techniques.
3. A consensus is reached on a solution to the problem in terms of the needs of internal and external customers.
4. The consensual solution is implemented, and activities and responsibilities are assigned.
5. Evaluation of the implementation activities and work processes is undertaken using quality monitoring tools.
6. Follow up on the results is achieved through the CQI cycle and ongoing consensual team activities.

Once the consensus model was chosen by the Acme Hospital, the task became one of addressing the court order to return patients to the least restrictive environment available to them. The team

consensually agreed to further analyze the problem by using a
cause and effect diagram.

THE CAUSE AND EFFECT DIAGRAM

The cause and effect diagram allows the problem under consideration to be explored within the parameters of multiple categories.
The procedure followed in the implementation is outlined below.

Implementation of the Cause and Effect Diagram

1. Select an organizational problem (i.e., effect) for analysis.
2. Determine the major categories and subcategories of causes
   that contribute to the problem.
3. Design a cause and effect diagram.
4. With each category and subcategory of causes ask the question, Why?
5. Analyze the information generated in step 4 and plan for CQI.

An example of the cause and effect diagram relative to the Acme
Hospital is presented in Figure 4.1.
    Analysis of the cause and effect diagram draws attention to the
four major causes of the problem (i.e., people, methods, facilities,
and equipment) that account for the current situation, in other
words, factors or variables (effects) that act against patients returning to their "least restrictive" environment. The cause and effect
diagram identifies specific subcategories of causal factors or variables. A deeper level of analysis as to the root nature of the causes
is facilitated by raising the question of why in relation to each of
the variables (causes) identified within the various subcategories.

FIVE WHYS TOOL

Inherent in step 4 of the cause and effect diagram is a further
opportunity for analysis of the various categories of causes. An
extension of this step is the use of the "Five Whys" quality tool.
Swanson (1995) notes that the objective of the five whys technique
is "to identify root, or key causes. It is similar in concept to peeling
an onion, where each layer of causes leads to additional layers until

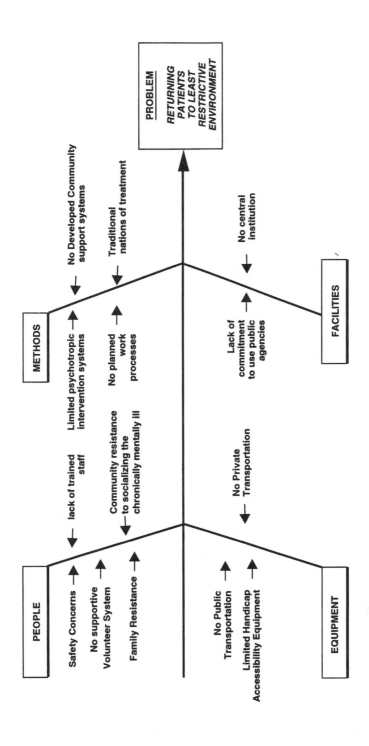

FIGURE 4.1 Cause and effect diagrams: Resource constraints mitigating against returning patients to their least restrictive environment.

37

the key causes are defined" (p. 121). Relative to the cause and effect diagram of the Acme Hospital, the team wanted to probe "why" there is community resistance to socializing chronically mentally ill patients into the community. The Acme Hospital, utilizing the five whys technique, probed this question in the following manner:

1. *Why* is there community resistance? Answer: Because there is fear of the chronically mentally ill.
2. *Why* is there fear? Answer: Because there is no understanding or tolerance of differences in the community toward the mentally ill.
3. *Why* is there no understanding or tolerance toward the chronically mentally ill? Answer: Because there have been no community education programs regarding mental illness in the community.
4. *Why* has there been no community education? Answer: Because there have been no organizational resources expended to develop an educational task force in the community.
5. *Why* has there been no organizational resources expended for an educational task force? Answer: Because no single human service organization has initiated leadership or coordination efforts in this area.

As can be seen, the five whys give depth and a greater understanding as to the nature and dimensions of the problem and provide some clarity to the tasks and work processes that will ultimately lead to problem resolution. It is clear that the data resulting from this type of *why* probing can lead to further, more complex analysis, a deeper understanding of the nature of root causes, and the quality processes intrinsic to effective change.

Implementation and Improvement of Work Processes

Once an analysis of the underlying root causes of a problem is completed, the work team can begin addressing the problem by specifying the work processes and sequence of activities needed to bring about quality improvement. Kinlaw (1992) has indicated that there are five major work process strategies that can address organizational problems. He catalogues these strategies as effective in accomplishing the following:

1. Responding to problems (malfunctions or breaks) as they occur.
2. Preventing the occurrence or reoccurrence of a problem by anticipating an event or by putting safeguards in place.

3. Upgrading some aspect of a process, e.g., computerizing a step or operation.
4. Experimenting by changing some aspect of a process and testing the results.
5. Creating a new process to replace an old one. (pp. 131–132)

Further, Kinlaw notes that work teams can measure improvements in these work process strategies in three ways:

1. Make the processes stable: Ensure that the distribution of the measures taken by the team to determine the performance of the process falls within limits or ranges that should be expected.
2. Reduce variation in the processes: Improve the process so that the distribution of measures that the team takes to determine the performance of the process comes closer and closer together, and therefore becomes closer to the average of the measure.
3. Improve the average: Move the total process to a higher level of performance so that the average of the measures that the team takes to determine the performance of the process becomes significantly higher or lower, depending on the desired direction. (pp. 132–133)

The Acme Hospital work team decided to respond to the lack of educational task groups in the community by creating and upgrading the number of work groups conducted on a weekly basis. The work team wanted to ensure that the number of educational groups was stable over time and that there was little variation in the training content across groups. In order to achieve this goal certain work process measurements were undertaken to ensure control of variation and stability.

WORK PROCESS MEASUREMENTS

In an effort to monitor the average number of work groups over time, the Acme team decided to obtain an average of the number of work groups conducted within the community over a 2-month period. In 1 month there were 15 educational groups conducted, and in another month 10 groups were conducted; therefore, the average number, called the mean, of educational groups was 12.5. The formula for completing the average is

$$\overline{X} = \frac{X_1 + X_2 + \ldots + X_n}{n} = \frac{15 + 10}{2} = 12.5,$$

where X_1 and X_2 are the measurements taken (i.e., number of educational groups) and n is the total number of measures taken (i.e., for 2 months).

Variation

Once an acceptable average (e.g., 12.5) is established, the Acme team will monitor the degree of variation in the number of educational groups being conducted monthly. Minimum variation is desired so as to ensure consistency in the offering of educational groups over time. The Acme team chose to use the range as a statistic to measure variation. The range is a statistic that measures the difference between the largest and the smallest values in a set of data. The formula for the range is

$$R = X_2 - X_1 = 15 - 10 = 5,$$

where X_2 is the largest value and X_1 is the smallest value. In the Acme case, the largest number of educational groups is 15 and the smallest number is 10; thus the range is 5. Other measures of variation that may be used include mode (the most frequently occurring value of the variable) and standard deviation (average deviation of the measurements [values] from the mean).

Stability

A measure of stability is desired by the Acme team so as to ensure predictability in the number of work groups offered over time. One manner in which stability can be measured is through the use of a run chart. Tague (1995) describes a run chart as "a graph that shows a measurement (on the vertical axis) against time (on the horizontal axis), with a reference line to show the average of the data." With reference to the Acme case, a run chart is represented in Figure 4.2.

The usefulness of the run chart lies in its ability to identify trends, patterns, and cycles. An obvious pattern seen in the Acme run chart is the trend for the number of groups being offered to diminish over time. Once trends are identified, work can begin on the appropriate processes to either maintain or change the situation.

Understanding key work processes is one of the primary concerns of a TQM initiative. An emphasis has been placed on the need to

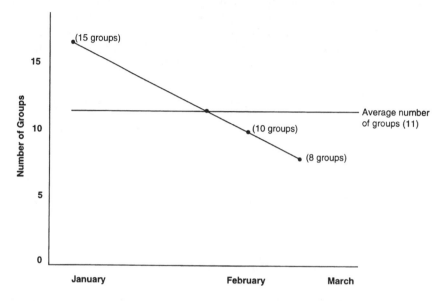

FIGURE 4.2 ACME Hospital run chart: Community educational groups.

produce quality results. The Acme case has presented some of the synergistic effects that can be realized from engaging in the analysis of work processes and team building. The opportunity for increased quality and enhanced performance offered by teams is readily accessible to human service organizations and well within the parameters of achievement for all management systems that emphasize CQI.

EXPERIENTIAL EXERCISE:
TEAM PROCESSES AND TQM DEVELOPMENT

Cause and Effect Diagram and the Five Whys

Activity 1

Have your group select a common problem or issue of concern that you have experienced in the workplace. Once you have decided on a problem or concern, either working alone or in pairs, construct a cause and effect diagram with four major causal categories and at least three subcategories. Once completed, rejoin your group and discuss the similarities and differences in the diagrams. Complete the construction of your personal cause and effect diagram in the space below.

Activity 2

Select a major causal category from the cause and effect diagram you have constructed and apply the five whys tool to this category. Write your five why questions and answers in the space below.

_____

_____

_____

_____

_____

_____

_____

_____

_____

_____

_____

_____

_____

_____

_____

_____

_____

_____

_____

_____

_____

_____

_____

_____

_____

_____

_____

_____

_____

_____

_____

_____

_____

Questions to Think About

What have you learned about the "root causes" of your problem? Briefly outline what you see as appropriate actions to remedy or resolve the problem.

_____

_____

_____

_____

_____

_____

_____

_____

_____

_____

_____

_____

_____

_____

_____

_____

REFERENCES

Gunther, J., & Hawkins, F. (1996). _Total quality management in human service organizations._ New York: Springer Publishing Company.

Oxford English Dictionary. (1978 ed.), s.v. "team."

Katzenbach, J. R., & Smith, D. K. (1993). _The wisdom of teams: Creating the high performance organization._ New York: Harper-Collins Publishers.

Kinlaw, D. C. (1992). _Continuous improvement and measurement for total quality: A team based approach._ San Diego, CA: Pffeiffer and Company and Homewood, IL: Business One Irwin. Copublished.

Schaaf, D., & Kaeter, M. (1992). _Pursuing total quality._ Minneapolis, MN: Lake Wood Publications.

Shonk, J. H. (1982). _Working in teams: A practical manual for improving work groups._ New York: AMACOM.

Swanson, R. C. (1995). _The quality improvement handbook: Team guide to tools and techniques._ Delray Beach, FL: St. Lucie Press.

Tague, N. R. (1995). _The quality toolbox._ Milwaukee, WI: ASQC Quality Press.

5

Group Interaction Tools and Pareto Analysis

On the journey toward continuous quality improvement (CQI) it is often difficult to know where to turn when problems are pressing from all sides. One of the strengths of the TQM paradigm is the clarity and confidence that can be fostered from the knowledge that, as a manager, one is not expected to solve the problems alone. Problem resolution within TQM is not simply the concern of management. Where there is a personal and organizational commitment to the ongoing pursuit of quality, it is the concern of everyone. Furthermore, effective problem solving within TQM is not seen as happening overnight. It takes time, effort, hard work, and planning. Joseph Juran (1989), one of the leading practitioners and theorists in TQM, identifies three key components of quality management, commonly referred to as the Juran trilogy: (1) quality planning, (2) quality control, and (3) quality improvement. These are viewed as processes that are not mutually exclusive; rather, they overlap and sometimes appear blurred in the press of daily activities that require the investment of energy and time.

Management within an organizational culture characterized by quality is different from traditional management paradigms driven by an unrelenting quest for ever higher levels of productivity. Not that productivity is unimportant, it isn't. It is important, however, within the context of a philosophy driven by an uncompromising concern for customer satisfaction, both within and outside the organization. This is why managers operating within a customer-driven culture of quality do not feel alone with the problems; there is a shared collectivist orientation and understanding that optimal decision making comes from teamwork and cooperation. Some managers will argue that such an orientation takes too much time and that many workers are not interested in having a larger voice in the running of the organization. There is little doubt that it takes time, but if it is done right the first time, the extra investment of time given at the beginning will have significant pay-off in the long run. Martin (1993) draws attention to Philip Crosby's key tenets of quality management, in which the importance of "doing things right the first time" is placed within the context of an organization-wide commitment to quality. He states it succinctly, "Raise quality awareness among employees by communicating what non-quality is costing" and underlines the importance of this principle in the action step: "Establish an ad hoc committee for a zero defects program" (Crosby, 1980, pp. 132–133).

The principles of TQM have proved to be effective in guiding the activities of organizations in the *for profit* corporate sector. In the process of becoming more customer oriented, these organizations have become more effective and efficient and ultimately more profitable in an increasingly competitive market. Organizations in the public sector are challenged to do better as well. Cohen and Brand (1993) state, "employees in the public sector are besieged on all sides by demands for productivity, quality and service" (p. 5). At the same time, one may be reminded that it is not a "magic solution" but rather the implementation of some fairly simple but key practices:

1. Working with suppliers to ensure that the supplies utilized in the work processes are designed for your use.
2. Continuous employee analysis of work processes to improve their functioning and reduce process variation.
3. Close communication with customers to identify and understand what they want and how they define quality. (pp. 5–6)

Cohen and Brand (1993) are clear in their prescription of where to begin in the mission to strengthen performance; it must begin with the client or customer, and they see the starting place as being on the front line, at the interface between internal and external customers. True to the principles of TQM, they identify step 1 as "have the workers describe and measure their work, and identify the work processes that should be improved, always beginning with the identification of customers and their needs" (p. 6).

To illustrate some of the tools of quality management and their application in the public sector, the Brixton Case, involving a large government department of social services, will be examined. Qualitative and quantitative decision making, group interaction, and problem resolution tools will be applied. They are as follows:

- Qualitative Tools: Nominal Group Technique
- Quantitative Tools: Pareto Chart

CASE: BRIXTON SOCIAL SERVICES DEPARTMENT

The Brixton Social Services Department is a large publicly funded multifunctional governmental organization going through a period of rapid change and transition. The 430 direct-service employees operate in 1 of 45 community district offices. Geographically dispersed, the offices, each with a district manager, serve primarily a rural population engaged in aquaculture and small-scale farming. District office managers report to one of four regional managers who are directly accountable to an executive team consisting of a chief executive officer, two assistant deputies, and five program directors. Traditionally, the government has operated on the basis of deficit financing but the debt has become so large that it can no longer continue the level of financial support to programs as in the past. In an attempt to address this problem and ultimately balance the budget, the government has directed all departments to commence an internal review of their operational mandate, service delivery structure, programming, and costs with a view to restructuring services and reducing overall costs by 20% over the next 18 months.

As a prelude to solving problems, the district managers decided to embrace the *nominal group technique* (NGT) interaction tool to get a sense of the prioritized problems as seen by their internal customers. This technique was chosen so as to give all workers an equal voice in the prioritizing of problems. Following the application of the NGT the managers decided to conduct a Pareto analysis. This type of analysis is designed to focus on the most critical problems and eliminate the trivial ones.

NOMINAL GROUP TECHNIQUE

One of the difficulties frequently experienced by professionals when working together and involved in diverse tasks and responsibilities is finding a consensus or common ground on what are the most important problems and which problems should be addressed first. This is particularly true for large organizations with employees who may be geographically dispersed. The case of Brixton Social Services is very similar, with its myriad problems and large employee population. The district managers faced an important question: "Where do we begin?"

NGT is a quality tool that can be used in a group to generate ideas and ultimately make decisions based on a consensus of support for the decisions reached. As a quality tool it operationalizes a major tenet of TQM: commitment to customers through a process of seeking out individual views, ideas, and concerns and processing them within a framework of CQI. It is particularly useful under circumstances as described in the Brixton Social Services case because of the size and diversity of staff. Kanji and Asher (1996) describe it as a good technique to use when someone (group or individual) may be dominating the situation. NGT gives a voice to all participants, encouraging a sense of ownership in the final outcome.

The Brixton district manager group realized that it was facing a number of important problems. The district managers decided that a necessary first step was to conduct an NGT process in order to accomplish the following four objectives: (1) promote participation on the part of all employees in a problem-resolution strategy, (2) foster a greater sense of individual and group understanding as to the nature of the concerns felt by fellow employees, (3) develop a sense of empowerment through the process of group participation, and (4) obtain a group consensus as to which problems are viewed as most important as the basis upon which to take further quality initiatives.

In the discussion that proceeded this decision, district managers acknowledged the importance of obtaining a divergence of views before bringing closure on the question of what is the most important issue or what problem should we tackle first? In taking this course of action, the managers generated a large number of ideas as a basis to pursue convergence and ultimately consensus. In this vein, Ebel (1991) describes the NGT as a "divergent-convergent technique for creating a large number of ideas and effectively ranking their importance" (p. 130).

Some district managers had used the technique before; others were not familiar with the basic steps or procedures to be followed. As a consequence, an internal trainer from Government Support

Services was selected to review the procedures with the group in a 1-hour training session. The thrust of this initiative was to plan and facilitate a series of individual district office workshops with staff for the purpose of developing a consensus about the problems to be given priority within Brixton Social Services. The procedures adopted for the nominal group meeting are outlined below.

Implementation Procedures for the NGT

- All ideas are to be written down on 3- x 5-inch cards without any personal identification as to the author.
- All members are to write down their own ideas on the cards independently without interacting with colleagues.
- The cards are collected and shuffled by the group facilitator and redistributed to each member.
- Each member is asked to take the idea written on the index card and with a felt-tip marker print it neatly on a flip chart in full view of the group.
- Members can work at the same time, so that others are invited to take their turn in printing the ideas from their cards on flip charts at the front. Participants are asked to make sure that no more than six ideas are written on each flip chart.
- When all of the ideas have been written on flip charts at the front of the room, members are invited to ask questions, provide clarification where appropriate, and suggest combining ideas that overlap or are the same. The group leader makes appropriate changes on the flip chart.
- Each group member is invited to copy on a clean sheet of paper the four most important ideas (issues listed on the flip charts at the front of the room). Rank each in order of priority, and assign a value of 3 to the most important, a value of 2 to the next most important, and a value of 1 to the lowest ranked idea.
- When this is completed, group members are asked to record their scores after the idea listed on the appropriate flip chart at the front of the room.
- The group leader adds up the scores for the items selected and rank orders them from the highest to the lowest scores.
- Items ranked in the top three are selected for priority action.

Following this format, the district office employees participated in an NGT workshop and identified a number of concerns. The

results of the district office rankings were tabulated into an aggre-
gate set of scores, and the information was faxed to all the district
offices. Based on the information obtained through the NGT, management concluded that the following four areas should be given
priority in terms of problem-solving activity:

1. Employee morale is low, and there is a widespread sense of
    insecurity related to an expectation that jobs may be cut.
2. A new registration act for social workers makes it mandatory
    that individuals occupying positions formally classified as
    social work have professional qualifications in social work at
    a minimum of the baccalaureate level. However, 25% of cur-
    rent social work positions are occupied by persons with less
    than the required qualifications.
3. High levels of stress are currently being experienced by work-
    ers in the area of child protection, related to higher caseloads
    and insufficient resources to meet the increasing number
    of referrals.
4. Clients with special needs related to physical or mental disa-
    bilities are dissatisfied with service accessibility related to
    the current lengthy waiting list.

Following from aggregation of data in the nominal group meeting
(Table 5.1) it was decided to conduct a Pareto analysis.

PARETO CHART—ANALYSIS

Mears (1995) defines a Pareto chart or analysis as "a way of organizing data that visually highlights categories for more detailed study.

TABLE 5.1 Brixton Social Services Cutback/Restructuring Problems

Issue Categories	Number of Responses	Cumulative of Responses	Cumulative Percentage
Low employee morale	90	90	45
Less than minimum social work qualifications	70	160	80
High caseloads	30	190	95
Client dissatisfaction	10	200	100
Totals	200		

That is, the diagram shows the major factors that make up the subject being analysed" (p. 90). A Pareto analysis separates the *critical few* problems that an organization should be working on from the *trivial many* that organizations usually work on. A Pareto analysis is based on the Pareto principle that states "that the large percentage of the results is caused by a small percentage of the causes. This is sometimes referred to as the 80/20 rule. An example of this rule is twenty percent of the errors produces 80 percent of the scrap" (Saylor, 1992, p. 116).

In constructing a Pareto chart, Kanji and Asher (1996) suggest the following operational steps:

1. List the activities or causes in a table and count the number of times each occurs.
2. Place these in descending order of magnitude in the table.
3. Calculate the total for the whole list.
4. Calculate the percentage of the total that each cause represents.
5. Draw a Pareto diagram with the vertical axis showing the percentage and the horizontal axis the activity or cause. The cumulative curve can be drawn to show the cumulative percentage from all causes.
6. Interpret the results. (p. 58)

The use of a Pareto analysis in the Brixton case (Figure 5.1) revealed that 80% of the organization's issues were related to two categories of problems: low employee moral and employees not meeting minimum social work qualifications. By identifying these two priority issues, Brixton Social Services was able to focus its attention on the internal processes and issues that were causing 80% of the problems. Thus they were able to initiate steps to address the concerns of its internal customers in a cycle of CQI.

EXPERIENTIAL EXERCISE: GROUP INTERACTION TOOLS AND PARETO ANALYSIS

This chapter has highlighted the group interactional tool of NGT and the use of the Pareto chart as an analytic tool that prioritizes problems in an organization. The information generated from such a process provides the basis for a problem resolution process and at the same time promotes a sense of customer ownership. From a prioritized list it is only a short step to frame the problem into a quality resolution

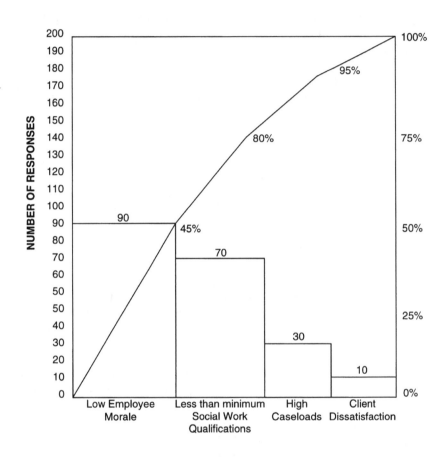

ORGANIZATIONALS PROBLEMS

FIGURE 5.1   Brixton Social Services cutback/restructuring problems.

process. The following experiential exercise is designed to assist in the mastery of these tools.

Experiential Exercise

In groups of five people, use the implementation process of the NGT to construct a cumulative percentage table that identifies the causes of job stress in the workplace. Enter your responses below.

Causes of Stress	Number of Responses	Cumulative of Responses	Cumulative Percentage
1.			
2.			
3.			
4.			
5.			
6.			
Totals			

Based on the cumulative percentage chart that you have developed, construct a Pareto chart and do a Pareto analysis. Does your chart illustrate the 80/20 rule?

What processes would you initiate in a human service organization to address the problems related to job stress? Enter your responses below.

_____

_____

_____

_____

_____

_____

_____

_____

_____

_____

_____

_____

_____

_____

_____

_____

_____

_____

_____

_____

_____

_____

REFERENCES

Cohen, S., & Brand, R. (1993). *Total quality management in government: A practical guide for the real world.* San Francisco: Jossey-Bass Publishers.

Crosby, P. (1980). *Quality is free.* New York: Mentor.

Ebel, K. E. (1991). *Achieving excellence in business: A practical guide to the total quality transformation process.* New York: Quality Press.

Juran, J. M. (1989). *Juran on leadership for quality: An executive handbook.* New York: Free Press.

Kanji, G. K., & Asher, M. (1996). *100 methods for total quality management.* Thousand Oaks, CA: Sage.

Martin, L. L. (1993). *Total quality management in human service organizations.* Thousand Oaks, CA: Sage.

Mears, P. (1995). *Quality improvement tools and techniques.* New York: McGraw-Hill.

Saylor, J. H. (1992). *TQM field manual.* New York: McGraw-Hill.

6

Problem Identification and Problem Analysis Tools

The ultimate mission of a human service organization is to provide the customer with a quality experience when using its services. In establishing a culture of quality, it is imperative for employees in human service organizations to begin "thinking quality." To begin this process, it is appropriate to redefine the client as the customer of the organization. This redefinition is essential if human service organizations are going to move their services toward a culture of quality and away from a strict culture of productivity. Patterson and Marks (1992) stress the importance of this redefinition by noting, "The term client conveys an image of an active professional in a paternalistic role and a passive consumer, whereas the term customer conveys an image of an active consumer selecting or purchasing a service or product" (p. 17).

Barrett (1994) also emphasizes the importance of achieving a customer focus in a human service organization when he notes that "Research conducted by the Strategic Planning Institute revealed that companies that outperform their peers in quality and customer satisfaction have profit margins of 12 percent versus 1 percent for their less customer-oriented competitors, and growth rates of 10 percent versus

0 percent" (p. 48). Once a customer focus is established within a human service organization, the TQM process can begin. Barrett (1994) again stresses this point by stating, "The force behind quality is a drive for excellence. The drive for excellence will not satisfy itself with quality only in some areas but seeks quality in all. That's what the *total* in *total quality management* means" (p. 32).

Striving for excellence in customer focus means that problems that block movement toward CQI must be identified and analyzed. Once problems are identified and analyzed, proactive strategies rather than reactive responses can be developed. In developing proactive strategies, it is important to include those individuals who are primarily affected by the problem. This inclusion not only operationalizes a basic tenet of the TQM philosophy but also is central and necessary to an effective problem-resolution initiative.

Problem-solving tools are necessary to effectively address a human service organization's quality problems. Problem-solving tools in TQM are qualitative and quantitative techniques used to achieve customer satisfaction. This chapter will examine the quality tools of flow charting and brainstorming and the application of scatter diagrams. These tools will be used in relation to the Donna case study.

CASE: DONNA

Bob and Anne, a middle-aged married couple, took Anne's 80-year-old mother, Donna, into their home to live with them after the recent death of her husband of 50 years. As a result, Donna was moved a thousand miles from her home of 35 years. She is on psychotropic medication to control a long-term cognitive disorder and smokes three packages of cigarettes a day. Within the last year she has had surgery for a stomach aneurism.

Confronted with Donna's myriad complex physical, social, and psychological problems, Bob and Anne decided that their first concern should be Donna's health care. Donna has limited funds and is a Social Security recipient, with health care provided under Medicare. Given this situation, Anne, as Donna's legal guardian, decided to enroll her in the care of a capitated Health Maintenance Organization (HMO). As an HMO member, Donna is required to have a baseline health assessment. Bob and Anne arranged for Donna's initial appointment. At the HMO office, they were greeted by an attendant, who gave Donna a checklist to note her current psychological conditions and other health problems. Donna did not understand the vocabulary on the form, so Bob and Anne helped her. Finally, after a 90-minute delay, Donna met the HMO physician, Dr. Smith. He asked Donna how she felt. After Donna replied that she was feeling okay, he quickly dismissed her without taking any laboratory tests or inquiring about her psychosocial status or other various ailments. Bob and Anne questioned Dr. Smith regarding this cursory assessment and were quickly dismissed with the comment "if any conditions arise you should bring Donna back."

Bob and Anne left the HMO frustrated and within a week withdrew Donna's membership from the program. They told their friends and relatives that they felt very disempowered from their experience with the HMO, and that, in their view, they were given extremely poor service. Finally, Bob and Anne wrote a letter of complaint to Mr. Charles, the organization's chief executive officer (CEO). Mr. Charles has noted that complaints about the program's services have increased over the last quarter and that there has been a corresponding drop in membership enrollment.

PROBLEM IDENTIFICATION TOOLS

Several tools are used to identify quality problems within an organization. This section will consider three quality tools within the context of the Donna case. These are:

1.   Flowcharting
2.   Brainstorming
3.   Use of scatter diagrams

The basic purpose of a problem identification tool is to give focus to the problem areas under review so that a clear problem statement can be developed. Once this statement is developed, a problem analysis can be initiated. One tool that can be helpful in this process is the flowchart.

FLOWCHART

A flowchart is designed to visually display all the processes involved in a particular organizational sequence. Symbols represent the sequence involved in these processes and their interactional relationships with each other. The major symbols used to visually display organizational processes in flowcharts include the following: process symbols, input and output symbols, decision symbols, start and finish symbols, document symbols, and directional symbols.

Martin (1993) notes a set of common questions, developed by Sheer (1991), that should be asked once a system's major processes are identified. These questions include

1. What processes generate the most customer complaints?
2. What processes generate the most errors?
3. What processes appear unpredictable?
4. What processes contain bottlenecks where product or service flow slows down, creating queues and backlogs? (Martin, 1993, p. 57)

In the Donna case study, problems with the HMO processes became visible at the point of intake. There was an extensive wait by the customers in spite of the fact that they had an appointment. In addition, the psychosocial information was gathered in a cursory matter. The problem was then compounded by the impersonal manner of the attending physician. He gave only scant attention to Donna's health and psychosocial problems. The concerns of her family support system, Bob and Anne, were also minimized by the physician. As a result, they filed a written complaint to the CEO and dropped Donna's membership in the HMO. Figure 6.1 outlines these processes in a flowchart format with relevant symbols.

BRAINSTORMING

Once a problem process has been identified, as in the preceding case, quality tools can be used to begin analyzing a particular problem. Analyzing a problem process leads to greater precision in identifying the root causes of the problem. The identification of root causes leads toward an action phase as part of a CQI cycle.

Brainstorming is a qualitative quality tool that facilitates an effective analysis of problem processes. Brainstorming generates a variety of ideas and encourages involvement and creativity among organizational members. Normally the brainstorming process begins with ideas that are generated from a single question. The generation of ideas is bounded by strict guidelines, however. Brassard (1988) outlines these guidelines as follows:

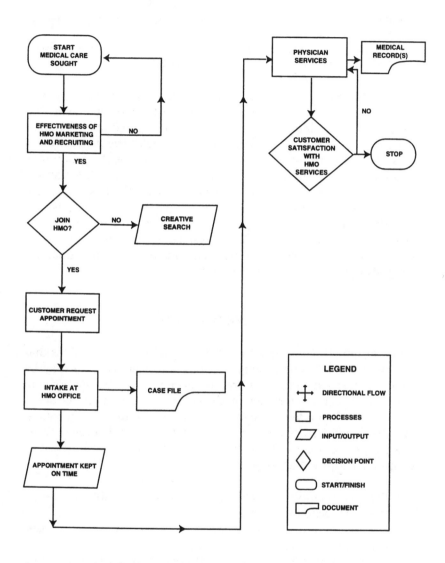

FIGURE 6.1 Flowchart: The Donna case.

- Never criticize ideas.
- Write every idea on a flip chart or blackboard. Having the words visible to everyone simultaneously avoids misunderstandings and reminds others of new ideas.

- Everyone should agree on the question or issue being brainstormed, and write it down.
- Record on the flip chart in the words of the speaker; do not interpret.
- Do it quickly; five to 15 minutes works well. (p. 69)

Brainstorming is a useful tool in the Donna case study. For example, through the earlier use of the flowchart, it became clear that the processes dealing with physician services and intake were particularly troublesome. After brainstorming, with the generation of ideas on "why" these processes were troublesome, the group may hypothesize that the longer a customer is kept waiting for an appointment, the higher will be the level of customer dissatisfaction. Another hypothesis could be that the longer the time the physician spends with a customer, the higher the level of satisfaction the customer will feel toward the physician's services. These two hypotheses are suggested; other relationships may be apparent, suggesting the need for further analysis.

SCATTER DIAGRAM

To determine the nature of the relationship between variables that emerge from a brainstorming session, a scatter diagram may be used. A scatter diagram is a graph that measures the relationship between two characteristics or variables. The graph has x- and y-axes. The independent, or causal, variable is plotted on the x-axis, and the dependent variable is plotted on the y-axis. There are three basic types of relationships that may be illustrated with a scatter diagram. These are as follows:

- Positive relationships indicate that as one variable increases, the other also increases.
- Negative relationships indicate that as one variable increases, the other decreases.
- Zero relationships indicate that there is no discernible relationship between the two variables under observation.

To construct a scatter diagram, certain steps must be taken. These steps are

1. Select the independent and dependent variables to be analyzed

2. Plot the independent variable on the x-axis of the graph and the dependent variable on the y-axis
3. Collect data on a suggested minimum of 30 cases
4. Plot the data
5. Interpret the direction of the plotted relationship and determine whether it is positive, negative, or zero by analyzing the scattered pattern that has been plotted

The two scatter diagrams in Figures 6.2 and 6.3 represent organizational concerns in the Donna case study. These or similar issues may arise in other organizational settings.

Figure 6.2 shows that there is a negative relationship between the length of time the customer is kept waiting and the level of

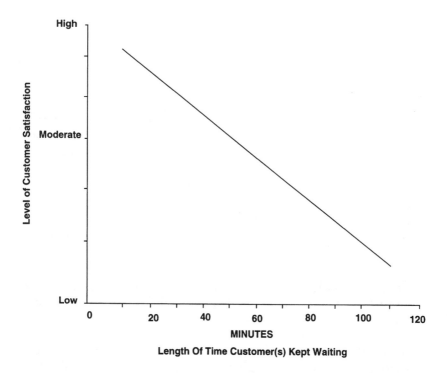

FIGURE 6.2   Length of time customer(s) are waiting and level of customer satisfaction.

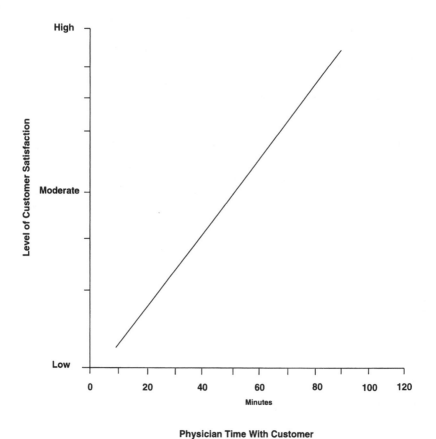

FIGURE 6.3   Physician time with customer and customer satisfaction.

satisfaction with a health service organization. In summary, the shorter the patient waiting period, the higher the level of satisfaction experienced by the customer.

Alternatively, Figure 6.3 indicates a positive relationship between the length of time a physician spends with the customer and the customer's level of satisfaction with the health service organization. Specifically, the longer the time the patient spends with the physician, the higher their level of satisfaction with the health service organization.

A scatter diagram is a valuable quality tool that can be used to validate the "intuitions" of a brainstorming group. In the Donna case study, the two hypotheses of the brainstorming group were confirmed. As a quality strategy, it may be helpful to return to brainstorming responses to the question as to why the relationships plotted out as they did.

EXPERIENTIAL EXERCISE:
APPLICATION OF QUALITY TOOLS

Flowcharts, Brainstorming, and Scatter Diagrams

This chapter has illustrated the use of three quality tools in identifying and analyzing organizational problems. Mastering these techniques takes practice, but it is important in establishing a personal process of CQI.

To facilitate personal mastery of these techniques, try the following experiential exercise. With a group of five people, share some of your personal stories about problems you have encountered with human service organizations. Select one story and, as a group, create a flowchart to illustrate all of the organizational processes involved with this problem. In creating the flowchart, use all of the symbols listed in Figure 6.1. Enter your flowchart in the space provided below.

Now that you have created a flowchart, select a leader to facilitate the brainstorming process. Then, have the group brainstorm as many ideas as possible about what factors may be included in the list of root causes that played a part in the breakdowns of organizational processes noted earlier in your flowchart. Follow the principles of brainstorming as outlined by Brassard (1988). Enter your ideas in the space provided below.

_____

_____
_____
_____
_____
_____
_____
_____
_____
_____
_____
_____
_____
_____
_____
_____
_____
_____
_____
_____
_____
_____
_____
_____
_____
_____
_____
_____
_____
_____
_____
_____

When your brainstorming session has concluded, construct a scatter diagram. This will illustrate the relationship between the variables that your group sees as being at the root of the identified problem. In this case, do an informal survey among yourselves. Plot the responses of your group and interpret the relationship between the two variables that have been selected for analysis. Enter your responses in the space provided.

Finally, in relation to the organizational problem that you have identified and analyzed, answer the following three questions:

- What happened in this problem situation?
- Why did this problem occur?
- What do you think will happen next? (i.e., How can this problem be resolved?)

Enter your responses in the space provided below.

_____

_____
_____
_____
_____
_____
_____
_____
_____
_____
_____
_____
_____
_____
_____
_____
_____
_____

REFERENCES

Barrett, D. (1994). *Fast focus on TQM: A concise guide to companywide learning.* Portland, OR: Productivity Press.

Brassard, M. (1988). *The memory jogger: A pocket guide to tools for continuous improvement.* Methuen, MA: Goal/QPC.

Martin, L. (1993). *Total quality management in human service organizations.* Newbury Park, CA: Sage.

Patterson, J. B., & Marks, C. (1992). The client as customer: Achieving service quality and customer satisfaction in rehabilitation. *Journal of Rehabilitation,* October–December, 16–21.

Sheer, L. (1991). Quality in higher education [Monograph]. Lawrence, KS: University of Kansas School of Business.

7

Work Process
Improvement Tools

Customer focus is the hallmark of TQM. Yet, there are many times in an organization when two competing service methodologies yield equal levels of satisfaction among consumers. Although it is true that both methodologies may be equally effective, a human service organization, in offering dual service delivery systems, may be presenting to the community a *lack of constancy of purpose.* Constancy of purpose is defined as the continuous quest for improvement coming from a clear sense of mission. Deming (1986) views this lack of constancy as one of the seven deadly diseases to which an organization can succumb. Capezio and Morehouse (1992) capture the organizational and social costs associated with this "deadly disease." They note that:

> When a [human service organization] has no constancy of purpose, no long range plans exist, managers and employees are often insecure and customers are often confused. Everyone wonders what they are supposed to be doing well. What is the plan for staying in business? For what purpose is the business organized? This information is significant throughout all departments and in every work group of a HSO. (p. 82)

Quality service in human service organizations demands that there be a consistent focus in service delivery to meet customer needs. If a human service organization is to maintain a clear vision of its services and engage in CQI, it must avoid ambiguity and communicate clearly to its internal and external customer base.

To promote clarity in service delivery, human service organizations will find the quality tools of focus groups and decision matrices helpful. The Leesville Community Mental Health Center case illustrates the application of these tools.

CASE: LEESVILLE COMMUNITY MENTAL HEALTH CENTER

The Leesville Community Mental Health Center (LCMHC) has existed in the suburban community of Leesville for more than 35 years. The primary mission of the center is to provide quality mental health services to the Leesville community. For the first 30 years of its existence, the center used a therapeutic intervention model that stressed the interventions of psychodynamic psychology as its primary service methodology. This service method was rated highly by the customers of the center. In the last 5 years, however, the demographics of the Leesville community have changed dramatically. The community's residents are now younger and more racially and ethnically diverse, and the average family income has fallen. In response to these changing demographics, the center has added short-term counseling and community-based primary prevention methodologies to its service delivery system. These services are also receiving high customer satisfaction ratings. The center faces a severe cut in its funding base, however, and can no longer afford its dual service methodology approach.

DECISION-MAKING QUALITY TOOLS

The LCMHC has decided that in order to address its funding dilemma, service delivery must become the focus of attention. At the same time, it was imperative that the Center maintain a clear sense of mission and a constancy of purpose for improvement. It is within this context of satisfied customers and constancy of purpose that a major decision had to be made, in other words, "what service delivery intervention mode would be maintained?"

FOCUS GROUPS

As a first step in addressing the current problem, the board of LCMHC decided to explore the issue through the use of focus groups and involve key customer informants in the community. Through this initiative, the board was able to generate relevant information as a basis for developing a decision-making matrix and thus bring a successful resolution to its service delivery dilemma. Tropman (1995) has defined a focus group as

> ... a specially assembled collection of people who can respond, through a semi-structured or structured discussion, to the concerns and interests of the assessor. Members of the group are invited and encouraged to bring up their own ideas and issues. Often the focus group is asked to test reactions to alternative approaches to an issue ... it is possible to have a focus group composed of key informants.... (p. 567)

The key informants selected for participation in the LCMHC focus groups included equal numbers of customers from each of the three service delivery methodologies offered at the center (i.e., psychodynamic, short-term counseling, and prevention services).

Stewart and Shamdasani (1990) enumerate a list of advantages derived from the use of focus groups. These advantages are as follows:

1. Focus groups provide data from a group of people much more quickly and at less cost than would be the case if each individual were interviewed separately.
2. Focus groups allow the researcher to interact more directly with respondents.
3. The open response format of a focus group provides an opportunity to obtain large and rich amounts of data in the respondents' own words.
4. Focus groups allow respondents to react to and build upon the responses of other group members.
5. Focus groups are very flexible. They can be used to examine a wide range of topics with a variety of individuals and a variety of settings.
6. Focus groups may be one of the few research tools available for obtaining data from children or from individuals who are not particularly literate.
7. The results of a focus group are easy to understand. Researchers and decision makers can readily understand the verbal responses of most respondents. This is not always the case with more sophisticated survey research that employs complex statistical analysis. (p. 16)

Implementation Procedure

The LCMHC used the focus group to establish criteria that could be incorporated within a decision-making matrix and thus facilitate their decision making. The Center used the following implementation process:

1. Establish a clear research focus and select a focus group leader.
2. Select focus group participants who are representative of an appropriate sample of customer groups relative to the information you wish to receive.
3. Develop a focus group interview schedule.
4. Analyze the focus group data.*
5. Report the data to key constituencies.

DECISION MATRIX

Results of the center's focus group indicated that several key criteria needed to be interfaced into a decision-making matrix. Key criteria included effectiveness, adequacy, cost, time, and capability. Tague (1995) describes a decision matrix as a tool that "evaluates and prioritizes a list of choices. The team first establishes a list of criteria and then evaluates each choice against those criteria" (p. 16).

Implementation Procedure

The implementation of a decision matrix involves the following procedure:

1. Identify the options and/or problems on which a decision needs to be made.
2. Select criteria against which the options or problems will be evaluated.

---

*Remember, data analysis need not be complex. Stewart and Shamdasani (1990) emphasize this point: "the most common purpose of the focus group interview is for an in-depth exploration of a topic about which little is known. For such exploratory research a simple descriptive narrative is quite appropriate. More detailed analysis simply are not necessary or efficient" (p. 102).

3. Weight each criteria and develop a rating scale for each criteria.
4. Develop an interactional impact matrix consisting of the options or problems and criteria.
5. Vertically and horizontally analyze the impact matrix.
6. Make decisions based on the weighted scores and qualitative discussion.

LCMHC developed a decision matrix from the information generated in the focus group sessions (Table 7.1).

In examining the LCMHC decision matrix, it can be seen that the human resource capability involved in the use of a psychodynamic intervention methodology at the Center is low. Such an approach requires highly trained physicians and specialists in psychiatry. Cost and time investment are viewed as high. Effectiveness is also seen as high, however. Short-term counseling costs rank as medium, whereas human resource capability and ultimate effectiveness rank high. Community-based preventive services are seen to have a low cost, with a medium ranking on effectiveness, time commitment and adequacy.

Based on the generation of these data and subsequent analysis, the board of the LCMHC decided to discontinue the use of a psychodynamic methodology and instead to limit their service options to short-term counseling and community-based preventive services.

TABLE 7.1 Decision Matrix—Leesville Community Mental Health Center: Service Delivery Methodologies

| | | SERVICE OPTIONS | | |
CRITERIA	WEIGHT	PSYCHO-DYNAMIC INTERVENTION METHODS	SHORT-TERM COUNSELING	COMMUNITY-BASED PREVENTIVE SERVICES
• COST	3	HIGH	MEDIUM	LOW
• TIME	3	HIGH	MEDIUM	MEDIUM
• EFFECTIVENESS	3	HIGH	HIGH	MEDIUM
• HUMAN RESOURCE CAPABILITY	2	LOW	HIGH	HIGH
• ADEQUACY	1	HIGH	MEDIUM	MEDIUM

Rating Scale: 1, Low; 2, Medium; 3, High

EXPERIENTIAL EXERCISE:
APPLICATION OF QUALITY TOOLS

Focus Groups and Decision Matrices

Clarity of focus and constancy of purpose in decision-making processes provide the foundation upon which quality can be operationalized. The experience of the LCMHC demonstrates the use of two quality tools in arriving at important service delivery decisions regarding the future. These tools can be applied in a variety of human service situations. The following exercise is intended to help your group develop the skills involved in focus group processing.

Focus Group Exercise:

Following the guidelines for implementing a focus group, form a focus group of six to eight people. Examine the following proposition and develop an interview schedule that explores the nature of the variables that give support to such a belief. Include in your interview schedule questions that probe how such a belief system can be effectively challenged.

> People on welfare prefer to avoid work and live off the government. Most welfare recipients are both lazy and irresponsible.

Enter your interview schedule here, noting what sample of people you would consider appropriate to interview.

_____
_____
_____
_____
_____
_____
_____
_____
_____
_____
_____
_____
_____
_____

From the interview schedule you have developed, assume a set of criteria that you might extract from the focus group research that accounts for this type of prejudice directed toward welfare recipients. From these criteria develop a decision-making matrix. Enter your decision matrix in the space provided below.

In relation to the decision-making matrix you have constructed, discuss your findings and list the final decision of your group here.

_____

_____

_____

_____

_____

_____

_____

_____

_____

_____

_____

_____

_____

_____

_____

_____

_____

_____

_____

_____

_____

_____

_____

_____

_____

_____

_____

_____

_____

_____

_____

_____

_____

_____

_____

_____

_____

Relative to the decision your group has made, answer the following questions:

1. What happened in your group in reaching the decisions that it did?
2. Why did your group make these decisions?
3. What will happen next? (i.e., what implications do you see as following from this decision?)

Enter your responses here.

_____
_____
_____
_____
_____
_____
_____
_____
_____
_____
_____
_____
_____
_____
_____
_____
_____
_____
_____

REFERENCES

Deming, W. E. (1986). *Out of the crisis*. Cambridge, MA: Massachusetts Institute of Technology, Center for Advanced Engineering Study.

Capezio, P., & Morehouse, D. (1992). *Total quality management*. Shawnee Mission, KS: National Press Publications.

Stewart, D. W., & Shamdasani, P. M. (1990). *Focus groups*. Newbury Park, CA: Sage.

Tague, N. R. (1995). *The quality toolbox*. Milwaukee, WI: ASQC Quality Press.

Tropman, J. E. (1995). Community needs assessment. In R. L. Edwards (Ed.), *Encyclopedia of social work* (19th ed., Vol. 1, pp. 563–569). Washington, DC: National Association of Social Workers.

8

Financial Management Tools

Typically, when dealing with the financing costs, procedures, and outcomes in human service organizations, administrators have used such tools as functional, zero-based, and line-item budgeting and cost systems. Used less often in the human services have been the financing, budgeting, and cost of quality tools that have been recently developed within TQM. Atkinson, Hamburg, and Ittner (1994) give emphasis to the point by noting that

> ... a common element within many of the successful companies is the use of more powerful *cost of poor quality* concepts in the selection and management of improvement projects that simultaneously improve financial performance and customer satisfaction. ... By offering customers higher quality and lower cost products, the Japanese added a new dimension to the idea of quality and changed customers' perceptions of superior quality from a defect free to superior value. (p. 57)

The notion of value does appear to be missing from human service organizations, particularly those operating in the public sector. Frequently, customers do not appear to value these services as they would services provided in the corporate sector. In order for human service organizations to gain a competitive edge, the services they offer must have "intrinsic" value to customers. Yates (1996) extended these propositions by calling for the development of a new type of human service manager, in other words, a scientist-manager-practitioner, one who is grounded in cost, procedure, and outcome analysis. He sees this new manager as achieving four essential goals:

- To continually improve the delivery of human services.
- To manage human service systems in an empirically accountable manner.
- To respond assertively and empirically to questions about effectiveness, benefit, cost-effectiveness and cost-benefit.
- To advance understanding of the origins, treatment and prevention of psychological, social and physical dysfunction. (p. 2)

The great challenge facing human service organizations today is to adapt, innovate, and change their ways of doing business and to bring about continuous quality improvements (CQI) and added value along the way. Here value is added to services whenever they are improved in a manner that enhances customer satisfaction. Berwick (1993) has noted that

> . . . our success in improvement will lie in the intersection of these new found and powerful methods, on the one hand, and the actual work we do on the other. If work does not change—if we do not change it—then TQM will be judged a fad, guaranteed. Should that happen, the sad error will not have been in total quality management, but in our commitment to change. (p. x)

The following case of the Newsboro Employment Agency will illustrate three new TQM financial management tools. These are customer-needs mapping, activity-based cost accounting, and customer-service loss calculation. Each tool supports human service organizations in their commitment to change and continuous quality improvement.

CASE: THE NEWSBORO EMPLOYMENT AGENCY CASE

Newsboro is a semi-rural area that has a poverty rate of 40%. Related to its high levels of poverty, Newsboro also has had a high level of unemployment. In order to implement an economic development initiative, the city council recently approved funding for the establishment of the Newsboro Employment Agency. The objective of the agency is to develop working relations with the private sector to promote higher levels of employment for area residents. Further, the city council mandated that the agency use a TQM financial management system to identify customer needs and to determine the costs associated with the various internal processes necessary to meet these needs. The internal processes that Newsboro Employment Agency selected to achieve its objectives are job assessment, job training, legislative advocacy, job placement counseling, information dissemination, and referral. Newsboro Employment Agency's external customer base consists of 200 private-sector employers.

FINANCIAL MANAGEMENT TOOLS

Any optimal financial management system for quality begins with strategic planning initiatives within the agency. In implementing and maintaining a customer-focused culture of quality within a human service organization it is important that the values promoting quality be maintained in the service mix associated with the agency. Additionally, the processes and costs associated with value-driven quality must be analyzed so as to eliminate those processes that are not congruent with the overall strategic plan of the agency. Also, once a customer base is established, it is necessary to account for and cost out the losses that emerge from this customer base. The tools of customer-needs mapping, activity-based cost accounting, and determining the cost of losing a customer will be illustrated in this section. These tools are designed to demonstrate that quality and value can be incorporated into the financial processes of human service organizations.

Customer-Needs Mapping

Mears (1995) defines customer-needs mapping as "a technique used to identify customer wants and then to identify the internal processes to meet those wants" (p. 163). Associated with this tool is the five-step process outlined below:

1. Customers for an agency process are identified.
2. A list of internal and external customer wants is developed.
3. Agency processes to meet a customer's wants are identified.
4. The importance of each customer need is rated using a rating scale where needs are rated from 1 to 5, 1 being least important, to 5 being the most important.

5. The effectiveness of each process in meeting the needs of customers is evaluated, in other words, rated as high (H), medium (M), or low (L) effectiveness. (Mears, 1995, pp. 163–164)

Table 8.1 illustrates the customer-needs map of the Newsboro Employment Agency. In identifying needs, the customers (i.e., 200 private-sector employers) discerned their needs to be: transportation, reliable workers, trained workers, employer tax credits, and employer child care tax credits. The effectiveness of the internal processes of the Newsboro Employment Agency in responding to customer needs is rated as high (H), medium (M), or low (L).

An analysis of the map in Table 8.1 shows the critical processes associated with external customer needs and the level of effectiveness of each. It can be seen that an employer tax credit or a child care tax credit that accrues to the private employer (external customer) is rated as a *high importance* need. Outside of assessing this need, however, there is a low level of effectiveness in meeting this customer requirement. Based on this information, activity-based cost accounting can be applied to these internal processes to determine how the development of resources can be used more effectively to achieve the desired benefits. For example, a costing of

TABLE 8.1 Newsboro Employment Agency: External Customer Needs Map

Customer Needs	Importance Rating	Customer Processes				
		Assessment	Training	Legislative Advocacy	On-Site Job Training	Resource Development
Transportation	3	H	L	L	L	L
Reliable Workers	4	H	H	L	L	L
Trained Workers	4	H	H	M	M	M
Employer Tax Credits	5	H	L	L	L	L
Employer Child Care Tax Credit	5	H	L	L	L	L

Effectiveness scale: H, High; M, Medium; L, Low

each of the customer processes related to the child care tax credit can be taken.

Activity-Based Cost Accounting

Activity-based cost accounting (ABC) is a relatively new quality management tool (Turney, 1991; Cortada, 1995). The primary function of this tool is to cost out the processes involved in a TQM undertaking. Cortada (1995) formally defines activity-based cost accounting as

> ... the body of accounting practices, sometimes also called a method by which one measures cost and performance of activities, processes, and cost objects. With such an approach, you can assign costs to activities or processes based on their use of such resources as people and supplies. A recognized by-product of activity-based cost accounting is the acknowledgement that there is a causal relationship between cost drivers and activities. (p. 253)

Forrest (1996) discusses how well activity-based cost accounting fits TQM. He notes,

> Under traditional costing systems, managers often made an error in judgement by assuming that work is driven by volume only. [Activity-based cost accounting] focuses its attention on the activities that cause work to happen and the activities performed in processing transactions which may or may not be volume-sensitive. (p. 333)

This end-to-end processing involved in activity-based cost accounting is supportive of TQM and its culture of quality. Forrest (1996, p. 334) delineates the cultural transformation that is needed to move from a traditional hierarchical culture to an activity-based cost accounting culture by noting that ABC is an open style with clear and concise objectives, encouraging group-derived continuous improvement.

Activity-based cost accounting can be applied to the Newsboro Employment Agency. A critical process meriting some attention is legislative advocacy. To apply activity-based cost accounting, the following five steps are necessary to determine:

1. Select a process in the agency to be costed
2. Define the activity steps in the process
3. Define the people and costs associated with the process

4. Assign a monetary value to each activity in the process
5. Establish the cost of activities associated with each step of the process

The following activities are seen to occur within the legislative advocacy process of the Newsboro Employment Agency:

- Identifying legislative advocacy issues (e.g., employer tax credits)
- Developing educational materials in relation to the targeted issue
- Educating key constituent groups in relation to the targeted issue
- Identifying and contacting key legislative leaders and advocating changes

Activity-based cost accounting involves the preparation of a detailed list of costs associated with each of the activities. For example, in step 3, salary costs are determined as a percentage of time allocated to the activity. In addition, supplies and related expenses associated with the activity, such as use of the photocopier, telephone, fax, computers, postage, and so on, are costed out. The result is a total financial accounting of the costs associated with the key processes within the human service organization.

Customer Service Loss Calculation

The importance of customer service and customer retention cannot be overstated in TQM. Customer service has the dual functions of providing necessary human and financial resources as well as the intangible asset of good will as strengthened through a satisfied customer base. A quotation from the world of business brings these important ideas into clear focus and can be readily extrapolated to human service organizations.

The average American company will lose 10 to 30 percent of its customers this year—mostly because of poor service. When customers have a choice, they'll go to the competition almost one-third of the time. If your customers don't have a choice—such as dealing with public utilities or government agencies—they'll use their feet for something else. They'll kick you. Customer dissatisfaction will erupt in the form of animosity directed toward your employees and your organization.

The psychological toll on your employees will result in higher absen-
teeism, turnover, stress-related illnesses and additional costs, as
burned out workers need to be retained or replaced. (Communication
Publications, 1990, p. 1)

Martin (1993) estimates a multiplier effect of 10 for human service
organizations that have dissatisfied customers. He sees this multiplier effect as a primary problem in human service organizations.

Given the importance of customer retention in human service
organizations, there has been little information on how to calculate
the cost of a lost customer in this context. Communication Publications has provided a guide to calculate the cost of a lost customer
(Figure 8.1). Although the guide relates primarily to sales-oriented
organizations, a ready translation can be made to the costs arising
out of the human service organization's activity-based cost accounting procedures.

In the case of the Newsboro Employment Agency, Figure 8.2 illustrates a method of calculating the cost of a lost customer (i.e.,
legislative system) arising from a private employer customer base.

---

1. Average or typical dollar amounts spent per day, week or month:$_____per day for legislative advocacy.

2. Annual dollar amounts spent:$_____.

3. Annual dollar amount x 18 (your lost customer plus the average number of others who may leave because of one customer's dissatisfaction): $_____ x 18 = $ _____.

4. Calculate the cost of replacing 18 customers ($118 is a typical annual cost per customer) : 18 x $__ _____.

5. Subtract the cost of keeping your present customer happy ($19 is a typical annual cost) from the cost of replacing 18 customers: $_____ - $_____ = $ _____.

6. Add the revenue- lost figure (step 3) plus the replacement costs (step 5):
$_____ + $_____ = $ _____.

This is a rough annual cost of your loss. Multiply by 10 to see what you stand to lose in a decade because of one lost customer.

FIGURE 8.1   Calculating the cost of a lost customer.

From *The Guide to Customer Service: Tips, Tactics and Techniques,* Briefings Publishing Group, 1101 King Street, Suite 110, Alexandria, VA 22314. Reprinted with permission.

The calculations in Figure 8.2, containing both tangible and intangible costs, identify the average cost of one lost customer to the Newsboro Employment Customer Agency. It becomes clear why human service organizations are frequently in a financial bind. Service to the customer is being overlooked!

EXPERIENTIAL EXERCISE:
APPLICATION OF TQM FINANCIAL TOOLS

There are several reasons why human service organizations should use TQM financial tools. Such tools give clarity to the actual costs associated with work processes or activities. They indicate the costs associated with losing a customer, and they make clear the needs of the agency's customer base. This chapter has presented the reasons for using financial tools and has illustrated the application of three specific tools: customer-needs mapping, activity-based cost accounting, and determining the cost of a lost customer for assessing the costs associated with a TQM initiative. The tools referenced in this chapter focus on customer

---

1. Average or typical dollar amounts spent per day, week or month:$ 100 per day for legislative advocacy.

2. Annual dollar amounts spent:$ 36,500 .

3. Annual dollar amount x 18 (your lost customer plus the average number of others who may leave because of one customer's dissatisfaction):
$ 36,500 x 18 = $ 657,000 .

4. Calculate the cost of replacing 18 customers ($118 is a typical annual cost per customer) : 18 x $ 2,124 .

5. Subtract the cost of keeping your present customer happy ($19 is a typical annual cost) from the cost of relacing 18 cust mers: $ 3,800 - $ 2,124   = $ 1,676 .

6. Add the reve ue- lost figure (step 3) plus the replacement costs (step 5):
$ 657,000 + $ 1,676 = $ 658,676 .

This is a rough estimate of annual cost of loss. Multiply by 10 to see what an organization stands to lose in ten years because of a single lost customer.

FIGURE 8.2   Calculating the cost of a lost customer in the Newsboro Employment Agency related to dissatisfaction—"legislative advocacy process."

service and the processes involved in promoting quality. The challenge is to master these tools. The following exercise will assist in this task.

Customer-Needs Mapping Exercise

Assume you are developing a child day care center for preschool children. Construct a customer-needs map for such an organization. Refer back to Table 8.1 and examine the structure of a needs map. Remember to include in your map (1) customer needs, (2) the "importance" rating for each customer need, (3) the internal agency processes that address customer needs, and (4) an effectiveness rating for each internal process of the center. Enter your map in the space provided below.

Cost-Activities Exercise

Once you have constructed your customer-needs map, select one internal process of the organization. Using the concepts of activity-based cost accounting, complete a costing of the activities associated with the process that you have selected. Enter your response in the space provided below.

_____

_____

_____

_____

_____

_____

_____

_____

_____

_____

_____

_____

_____

_____

_____

_____

_____

_____

_____

_____

_____

_____

_____

_____

_____

_____

_____

_____

_____

_____

_____

Calculating the Cost of a Lost Customer Exercise

Now assume that you have a customer base of approximately 100 children for your day care center. Based on this number of customers and the analysis you provided from applying your activity-based cost accounting tool, calculate the dollar cost of one lost customer. Use the calculation schema provided for you in Figure 8.1. Enter your calculations below.

CONCLUSION

Finally, in relation to the TQM financial tools that you have used and the problems of developing a child care agency, answer the following three questions:

- What financial problems occurred in relation to the work processes here?
- Why did these problems occur?
- What do you think will happen next in relation to these problems?

Enter your responses in the space provided below.

REFERENCES

Atkinson, H., Hamburg, J., & Ittner, C. (1994). *Linking quality to profits: Quality-based cost management.* Milwaukee, WI: ASQC Quality Press and Montville, NJ: Institute of Management Accountants.

Berwick, D. M. (1993). Foreword. In P. Hassen, *Rx for hospitals.* Toronto, Canada: Stoddart Publishing Co.

Communication Publications. (1990). *The guide to customer service: Tips, tactics, and techniques.* Blackwood, NJ: Author.

Cortada, J. W. (1995). *TQM for information systems management: Quality practices for continuous improvement.* New York: McGraw-Hill.

Forrest, E. (1996). *Activity-based management: A comprehensive implementation guide.* New York: McGraw-Hill.

Martin, L. (1993). *Total quality management in human service organizations.* Newbury Park, CA: Sage.

Mears, P. (1995). *Quality improvement tools and techniques.* New York: McGraw-Hill.

Turney, P. B. (1991). *Common cents: The ABC performance breakthrough.* Portland, OR: Cost Technology.

Yates, B. (1996). *Analysing costs, procedures, processes and outcomes in the human services.* Thousand Oaks, CA: Sage.

9

Benchmarking

Camp (1993) notes that "the Japanese word *dantotsu*, meaning striving to be the best of the best, captures the essence of benchmarking. Benchmarking is a positive proactive process to change operations in a structured fashion to achieve superior performance. The purpose of benchmarking is to ensure the probability of success in gaining a competitive advantage" (pp. 1–9.2).

It is important to note that the search for the "best practice" cannot be separated from the CQI cycle, an intrinsic component of TQM. Without the cycle of CQI there is no definitive customer, and another system of management should be explored. Within the context of a CQI process, benchmarking offers several advantages to human service organizations.

- It promotes and generates breakthrough thinking and innovation.
- It generates high levels of achievement motivation to become the best.
- It allows for global best practices to be adapted in a local organization.
- It enables both internal and external customers to obtain the best technology and methods available.

Mears (1995) has described five different types of benchmarking:

- Internal benchmarking occurs when a firm looks within its divisions or branches and compares repetitive operational functions.
- Competitive benchmarking involves identifying key competitive characteristics of a product or service and then comparing these characteristics to your competitors.
- Shadow benchmarking involves monitoring key product and service attributes of a successful competitor and meeting changes as they occur.
- Industrial benchmarking often called functional benchmarking involves a comparison of functions within the same industry.
- World Class benchmarking involves comparisons of processes across diverse industries. . . . That is, a comparison is made of your process to the best in the world, no matter what the industry. (pp. 155–156)

Each of these types of benchmarking may be seen as applicable to human service organizations. Given the current realities of resource constraints and funding cuts, however, it is appropriate to focus on a case involving the use of competitive benchmarking.

DEVELOPING A BENCHMARKING SYSTEM

It should be remembered that benchmarking is intrinsically linked to a customer focus. It should be assumed that before any benchmarking initiative is employed, an agency has identified its internal and external customers and its operational processes. Camp (1993) has developed a 10-step process with five essential phases that complements the CQI cycle of TQM (pp. 1-9.4–1-9.7). Figure 9.1 illustrates the model.

Although there is currently no list of the "best in a class" for human service organizations, human service managers can consult a list of the recent winners of the Malcolm Baldridge National Quality Awards to learn about "best process" for benchmarking purposes. To illustrate the application of benchmarking in a human service organization, the Mid City Settlement House case is presented.

CASE: THE MID CITY SETTLEMENT HOUSE

The City of Fairtree invited competitive bids on a proposal to develop a settlement house in its midcity area. The prospectus identified an expectation that the winning proposal would include a "breakthrough benchmark." Human Resources Inc. (HRI) submitted the winning proposal. They outlined the details of their plan to establish a community-based settlement house in midcity. The pur-

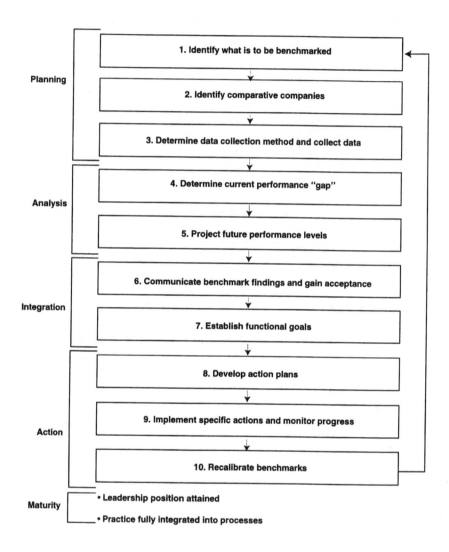

FIGURE 9.1   Benchmarking process steps.

From Benchmarking: The search for industry best practices that lead to superior results (p. 17) by R. C. Camp, 1993. In W. F. Christopher & C. G. Thor (Eds.) (1993), *Handbook for productivity measurements and improvements*. Portland, OR: Productivity Press. Reprinted with permission.

pose of the settlement house was to increase the quality of life for individuals living in this area. Increasing the quality of life was clarified in a set of service program objectives for Mid City Settlement House related to crime reduction, preservation of families, and increasing the provision of recreational activities and substance abuse counseling. The breakthrough benchmarking strategy offered by HRI, however, was a *negotiated service guarantee* with the city of Fairtree so as to reimburse a portion of the funding support if CQI was not demonstrated.

As indicated in Figure 9.1, the "five phases" of the benchmarking process include planning, analysis, integration, action, and maturity. In developing its winning proposal, HRI incorporated the following actions in their plan.

Planning

In responding to the city's objective to enhance the quality of life for citizens in the midcity area of Fairtree, HRI realized that its service proposal had to incorporate what they considered "best practice" in order to successfully meet their expectations. Given that HRI's internal service processes were integrated into a CQI cycle, the organization decided to benchmark its service process systems with other competitors. With this objective in place, data were collected and comparisons were made with competitors.

Analysis

Following the analysis of data in relation to competitors it was apparent that no significant performance gaps existed in the service processes of HRI. In fact, the evidence indicated that HRI's service system processes were of high quality. Although satisfied with these findings, HRI wanted to push even further to develop a value-added breakthrough practice to its service offerings. The decision was made to offer a negotiated service guarantee in the provision of a services agreement with the city. This involved a system of regular and systematic service reviews, with the city as external customer able to claim reimbursement for services not meeting specified standards or quality expectations.

Integration

Employees of HRI in formulating the specifics of the services guarantee to the city operationalized the performance levels viewed as necessary to satisfy the city's expectations. Benchmarking metrics provided baseline data on "quality of living" conditions in the mid-city area along with benchmark gaps where services were needed or were below standard. Once performance levels were established, internal service review processes were linked with appropriate service goals. Feedback measures incorporating a TQM CQI cycle were established and made part of the service guarantee finally negotiated with the city. Participation of all HRI employees in this phase promoted both understanding and commitment to the TQM initiative.

Action

The benchmark metrics operationalized through the CQI cycle provided the necessary process feedback to develop and produce a set of quality of life indicators for the city. Responsibility charts were constructed for all project participants, and regular progress reports were provided to all internal and external customers.

Maturity

The status of internal maturity will be achieved for HRI when its service guarantee is fully integrated into the statistical control processes of the organization. External maturity on the other hand will be achieved when its service guarantee is identified as a best practice in the field of human services.

This chapter has given a brief overview of the benchmarking process as it may be used in human service organizations. To facilitate benchmarking skills development, the following experiential exercise provides practice in the five phases of the benchmarking process.

EXPERIENTIAL EXERCISE: APPLICATION OF BENCHMARKING AND TQM

The purpose of benchmarking key processes within human service organizations is to identify and understand the nature of best practice(s). Assume that you are the director of a residential home for substance abusing adolescents. You have been asked to benchmark the counseling services that you are currently providing to these youths.

You have chosen to use Camp's benchmark process model (Figure 9.1) as a guide to your initiative. Before you implement the benchmarking process, describe and develop the service process that your residential home has for counseling. Complete the following activities and answer the following questions.

Plan

1. What are the best practices in regard to counseling substance abusing adolescents? You may want to consult professional journals on this point.
2. What service process would you choose to benchmark?

Write your answers in the space below.

_____

_____

_____

_____

_____

_____

_____

_____

_____

_____

_____

_____

_____

_____

_____

_____

_____

_____

_____

_____

_____

_____

_____

_____

_____

Now that you have gathered information, it is time to analyze that information.

Analysis

1. How does your residential substance abuse counseling process measure up to the other systems you have identified?
2. What is the gap between your services system and the other service systems you have identified?

Write your answers below.

_____
_____
_____
_____
_____
_____
_____
_____
_____
_____
_____
_____
_____
_____
_____
_____
_____
_____
_____
_____
_____
_____

After analyzing your data, your next task is to integrate your bench-marked process into your agency.

Integration

1. How could you incorporate the best practices you have identified into your current service processes?
2. What quality tools and measurements would you use to ensure CQI in your process?
3. How would you communicate to all of your customers the new service processes you are about to implement?

_____

_____

_____

_____

_____

_____

_____

_____

_____

_____

_____

_____

_____

_____

_____

_____

_____

_____

_____

_____

_____

_____

_____

_____

_____

_____

_____

_____

_____

After integration of your benchmarked processes action can now take place.

Action

1. What specific measurements and quality tools would you use to ensure CQI in your benchmarking process?
2. Who would be responsible for implementing the benchmarking findings?
3. How would progress be reported on the new system to all of your customers?

_____
_____
_____
_____
_____
_____
_____
_____
_____
_____
_____
_____

Maturity

1. What indicators would you look for to know that you have achieved a best practice status in your counseling service process? Write your answer in the space below.

_____
_____
_____
_____
_____
_____
_____
_____
_____
_____
_____

Finally, after completing your benchmarking process answer the following questions:

1. What problems are happening in your organization which could lead to a benchmarking initiative?
2. Why do you think these problems occurred?
3. What do you think will happen next (i.e., how will they be addressed)?

_____

_____

_____

_____

_____

_____

_____

_____

_____

_____

_____

_____

_____

_____

_____

_____

_____

_____

_____

_____

_____

_____

REFERENCES

Camp, R. C. (1993). Benchmarking: The search for industry best practices that lead to superior performance. In W. F. Christopher & C. G. Thor (Eds.), *Handbook for Productivity Measurements and Improvement* (pp. 1-9.1–1-9.12). Portland, OR: Productivity Press.

Mears, P. (1995). *Quality improvement tools and techniques.* New York: McGraw-Hill.

10

Charting the Future

Some elements of the TQM paradigm have been around for a long time. Walter A. Shewhart of the Bell Telephone Laboratories in the United States wrote about the application of statistics to measure product quality as far back as the 1920s (Mizuno, 1988, p. 281). Shewhart's famous work on quality control in industry titled *The Economic Control of Quality of Manufactured Products* introduced the control chart as an effective tool to measure variation in the processes of production (Shewhart, 1931). TQM as an integrated and holistic management system is quite new, however, having been introduced to the United States as late as 1981. Quite remarkably, in less than two decades it has radically changed the culture and focus of many organizations, both in this country and throughout the world. For these organizations it is no longer business as usual. A quality focus, with the hallmarks of customer service and satisfaction, is a top priority, evidenced by a fundamental shift in management thinking as to "how organizations should best be run."

The perceived benefits of TQM have varied from organization to organization. TQM is seen by some organizations as a means of gaining a competitive advantage in a marketplace marked by increasingly sophisticated customer populations and shifts in patterns of customer spending. Given the current realities of change, with its accompanying uncertainties, TQM has provided others with a management framework that has fostered a deeper understanding of the nature of organizational problems and how quality tools can play a role in their effective resolution. TQM will be viewed differently by different people. Not least important is recognition that TQM is a total systems approach to management and leadership. It is intrinsically proactive in its commitment to that sometimes elusive phenomena that is labeled quality. TQM moves employees forward, fostering a vision of new possibilities and resistance to the tendency of becoming preoccupied with the problems of the day. Effective planning from this perspective will recognize the importance of anticipating what the future may be. Charting the future may be seen as the challenge of this new management system in that visions of tomorrow become the work of today.

Unfortunately, some view TQM as a quick fix, a way around organization problems or a strategy that can be grafted to isolated elements of traditional management practice. Such an approach is doomed to failure from the beginning. The TQM paradigm is an all-encompassing management system that requires radical change at all levels of the organization. Hence the term *culture of quality*. Traditional management practices cannot coexist with an effective TQM paradigm because of a variation in focus, in other words, quality rather than productivity. This is not to say that productivity and other traditional concerns are not addressed within a TQM culture. They are addressed. In fact TQM is specifically concerned with issues related to the efficient and effective use of resources, but always from the perspective of the customer.

TQM is not a one-time process. It is a continual process, a way of running an organization that seeks neverending quality improvements. The key to this is the focus on the customer. The customers (internal and external) determine what quality is, not managers. An organization adopting TQM must employ the tools and tenets of such a system, not just to meet quality standards but also to reach for excellence. Of course customer needs and perceptions as to what constitutes quality or excellence are not static. They change over time. To achieve an effective cycle of CQI, there must be an organizational responsiveness to customers and their changing needs. It is within this context that quality tools become the means whereby work processes are subject to the scrutiny of a quality focus. Questions must be asked repeatedly: Is this a quality product or service? How do we really know that it is? In short, quality in terms of customer satisfaction must drive the organization in all of its activities.

In many ways not-for-profit human service organizations are unique in comparison with business organizations motivated by profit. Both types of organizations can benefit from the TQM paradigm, however. Frequently, human service organizations are funded or managed, or both, by government. In many instances, they represent a monopoly in their fields of practice or in the services they provide, with no market-oriented competitive pressures. This can lead to a spirit of complacency within the organization because there is less motivation to serve customers in terms of internal and external quality expectations. Organizational survival is frequently not at stake. In a profit-oriented organization the benefits of being at a level of top quality are realized in terms of the continuity and success of the business. Not for profit human service organizations cannot turn to the end of the year profit and loss statement to determine success. Nevertheless, the TQM paradigm offers a meaningful and effective antidote to this tendency toward complacency. Beginning with a commitment to customers, TQM challenges organizational members to think of all services from a quality best perspective.

At the same time, there is another type of competition that does apply to human service organizations. In a time of reduced government funding there exists competition among government-funded organizations for the scarce resources. An organization with a successful TQM culture that meets the quality needs of its customers and is able to demonstrate this can be viewed as holding a position of *competitive advantage* in the marketplace of scarce funding. In essence, the focus on quality, and achieving that quality, will make the organization or program more competitive in its bid for financing that is in short supply.

Team work and group management are another fundamental element of the TQM approach. Teams can provide a multitude of skills, knowledge, experiences, and judgments that are essential to making sound decisions throughout the quality improvement cycles. All customers, both external and internal, of an organization can identify avenues, issues, and concerns in the continuous pursuit of quality improvements. Traditional systems of management frequently leave this task to the imagination of managers, that is, to identify what is relevant in the process of problem solving, evaluation, or decision making. Often, managers are not in a position to see what is really going on and as a consequence are unaware of many opportunities that exist for problem prevention initiatives or overall enhancement of internal work processes. The team management participatory concepts inherent in the TQM paradigm draw on the knowledge, skills, and experiences of all organizational members. Such knowledge, skills, and frontline experience have frequently been overlooked or underused in traditional systems of management.

An organizational commitment to learning, skills development, and training of employees is an essential element of a TQM culture. This is particularly important in the implementation phase but does not end there. Successful TQM initiatives incorporate training for staff members at all levels after a careful assessment of the organization's needs and an evaluation of employee readiness. Measurement tools will provide the information with which to effectively plan a program of knowledge building and skills development in required areas. Beyond the immediate transitional training, the challenge of continuous learning must become an integral part of the day-to-day culture of the organization. Such a learning environment ensures a climate of responsiveness to the changing needs of customers and the social, political, economic, and technological realities that shape the workplace and the community. In short, an initial and ongoing program of learning is an integral part of TQM and reflects the high value placed on timely and effective responses to the changing needs of customers.

The work processes that organizations undertake to create, maintain, assess, and deliver quality products and services are in essence the backbone of an organization and ultimately determine the quality that a customer will receive. Ongoing monitoring, measurement, analysis, design, and redesign of the processes are fundamental to a culture of CQI. In fact, this may be seen as a central cornerstone of TQM because of the importance that is placed on the generation of reliable and valid information in planning and decision making. Deming (1986) stressed the importance of statistical measures in the implementation of internal quality control systems, process design, and redesign to ensure the achievement of quality. Quality improvements and quality analysis are based on statistics derived from processes that track the nature of changes and key activities both internal and external to the organization. This acknowledges the true nature of organizations as open systems, where service deficiencies or service excellence in one area will influence the nature of services in other areas.

TQM is grounded in a philosophical commitment or goal to achieve *zero defects*. This can only be achieved if the processes involved in the creation of various products and services are systematically and regularly monitored, measured, and analyzed. Variation in processes can only be understood against a backdrop of relevant information and a quality focus or goal that seeks to reduce deviation from quality expectations to zero. For some, such an expectation may be viewed as unrealistic, but it must not be forgotten that the maximization of quality, as defined by the customer, is still the primary goal. Stated differently, a quality best product with some variation is more desirable than a product with only moderate quality and little or no variation. In short, variation in quality in itself reduces the total quality of the products and services that are produced. For this reason, it simply cannot be ignored where quality is the goal.

THE TOOLS OF TQM: A REVIEW

PDCA

This tool assists in the process of controlling for quality in the workplace. It is helpful in detecting problems as they occur and preventing problems before they occur. This tool is designed to enhance work activities or processes so that quality in products and services is achieved. This process involves (1) recognizing opportunities and planning for necessary change in a timely manner, (2) testing the opportunity or plan on a small scale, (3) evaluating the results, and (4) taking appropriate actions based on the results and analysis of the test. From here the cycle begins again with the implementation of a larger-scale plan, based on the findings or going back to the drawing boards to devise a new plan.

Force Field Analysis

This tool assists in understanding the nature of organizational problems and the dynamics of variables or forces that push for change or work to support the status quo. In essence, it is a process analysis tool that focuses on the helping and the hindering forces in relation to the current situation and gives profile to the organization's sense of where it wishes to be in the future. This tool helps break down the problem into smaller and more manageable segments so that appropriate actions can be taken to bring about change.

Consensus Model

This tool assists in group discussion and decision-making processes through a step-by-step process of review and analysis of the problems and possible solutions. It is particularly useful in that it helps participants seek solutions that are sensitive to the needs of participants and values a win-win approach to problem resolution.

Cause and Effect Diagram

This tool assists in determining and understanding the root causes of a problem or process by graphically presenting the relevant variables (diagramming) and analyzing the major categories and subcategories of the causes.

Five Whys

This tool assists in determining the root causes in a problem or process by systematically exploring the nature of the problem or issue by asking *why,* successively, as deeper meaning and understanding is sought.

Work Process Measurement

This tool assists in the analysis of work processes in the organization through measuring various aspects of the processes, both inputs and outputs. This information becomes the basis for decisions on quality improvements in the way work is done or processes are accomplished. Averages, variation, and stability measures of different aspects of the processes compose the bulk of the information that is collected. Specific areas include responsiveness to problems and experimentation to determine the effects of changes to the process.

Flowcharting

This tool assists in analyzing work processes in an organization through the use of a visual display of the relevant processes and activities involved. This includes information flows, physical flows, decision points, and subprocesses. These diagrams, or variations of them, are used in a variety of fields, including the area of information technology design. This tool is helpful as a documentation and efficiency analysis tool.

Brainstorming

This tool assists work groups or teams in a process of idea generation by involving organizational members in a group discussion. In this context many free-flowing ideas are generated. This tool can facilitate creative problem analysis and novel approaches to resolution.

Scatter Diagram

This tool assists in determining correlation or cause and effect relationships through the use of an experimentation and case study to obtain data on key variables. Data is plotted on a graph to determine the nature of relationships between variables. Once the relationship is known appropriate actions can be taken to reach a desired effect (e.g., increase customer satisfaction).

Nominal Group Technique

This tool assists in the generation of ideas and decision making in a work group setting. The process involves group members independently and anonymously generating ideas and opinions which are collected and summarized for group viewing. Ideas are reviewed and ultimately short-listed in terms of what appears to be most important. This information is then used to prioritize information or ideas as a basis for further action.

Pareto Chart or Analysis

This tool assists in highlighting crucial factors that contribute to defects or problems in the operationalization of the 80-20 principle, in which 80% of the problems are seen to be generated by 20% of the factors or variables, in other words, the vital few. This analysis illuminates the causes of problems by identifying the critical variables that operate in the situation. Once the total problems emanating from a particular cause are tabulated, this tool facilitates the identification of the crucial causes (usually 20%) that create the problems (usually 80%).

Focus Groups

This tool assists in the generation of ideas regarding a particular situation, problem, or decisions. It involves the assembling of key informants or stakeholders in a type of roundtable semiformal discussion on problems or issues and possible solution alternatives. The key informants will normally represent the different views and concerns of internal and external stakeholders. This format of discussion provides an opportunity for all viewpoints to be addressed in a nonconfrontational way.

Decision Matrix

This tool assists team members in evaluating and prioritizing choices. Its value is seen in the generation of a variety of alternatives or solution strategies against the backdrop of a consensual set of relevant evaluative criteria (e.g., cost, time, effectiveness, etc.). This provides a rational basis for action steps and decision making.

Customer-Needs Mapping

This tool assists in identifying customer needs and the organizational processes that are intended to meet those needs. Use involves identifying all internal and external customers and ranking their needs by order of priority or importance. The processes involved in meeting customer needs are also ranked for effectiveness to give an overall chart or map of critical variables and associated activities.

Activity-Based Cost Accounting

This tool assists in determining the actual costs of processes associated with key events or activities (i.e., the production of products or services) within the context of a TQM initiative. The total financial cost is determined through a detailed analysis of work flows or activity steps to determine the nature and amount of resources that are consumed in accomplishing a particular objective. Actual dollar amounts are given to each unit of each resource that is consumed. This tool can also help identify the cost drivers that have an impact on variation in costs.

Customer Service Loss Calculation

This tool assists in identifying the cost of providing below-standard (subquality) products or services to a customer. The identification of the cost associated with not providing top quality products or services gives profile to the importance of a total quality culture. Lost customers represent a loss that is often hidden to the organization. This tool shows how losses can be calculated. The actual formula involves a simple mathematical calculation that gives focus to the erosion of an organization's customer base and psychological toll on employees.

Benchmarking

This tool assists in the analysis of organizational processes through the use of best practice comparisons both internal and external to the organization. Benchmarks provide a measure against which an organization can determine progress toward the attainment of quality goals. Organization processes can be benchmarked within functional areas of an organization, with other competitors, with accreditation standards, and with the *best in the world* practices of other human service organizations. This tool operationalizes quality criteria in the quest for CQI.

REFERENCES

Deming, W. E. (1986). *Out of the crisis.* Cambridge, MA: MIT Press.
Mizuno, S. (1988). *Company-wide total quality control.* Tokyo, Japan: Asian Productivity Organization.
Shewhart, W. A. (1980). *The economic control of quality of manufactured products.* American Society for Quality Control. [Original edition 1931, New York: Von Nostrand Reinhold].

Appendixes

Central Management Tenants of Crosby, Deming, and Juran

The primary developers of the quality movement that have influenced work within Canada and the United States have developed their own central tenets to quality management. The approaches of Phillip B. Crosby, W. Edwards Deming, and Joseph M. Juran are presented below.

PHILLIP B. CROSBY

1. Obtain management commitment
2. Form a quality improvement team
3. Determine the status of quality throughout the organization by quality measurement
4. Establish the cost of quality evaluation
5. Raise quality awareness among employees by communicating what nonquality is costing
6. Take corrective action on previously identified organizational problems

7. Establish an ad hoc committee for a zero defects program
8. Implement supervisor training with all levels of management in regards to the quality improvement program
9. Establish the performance standard of zero defects via a Zero Defects Day
10. Establish goals during meetings with all employees
11. Ask individuals to describe any problems that keeps them from performing error-free work
12. Recognize performance of participating individuals
13. Establish quality councils of participating individuals
14. Do the program steps over again to emphasize the continuous improvement (Crosby, 1979, pp. 132–139)

W. EDWARDS DEMING

1. Create consistency of purpose for improvement
2. Adopt the new philosophy
3. Cease dependence on mass inspection
4. End the practice of awarding business on price tag alone
5. Improve constantly and forever the system of production and service
6. Institute training
7. Institute leadership
8. Drive out fear
9. Break down barriers between staff areas
10. Eliminate slogans, exhortations, and targets for the workplace
11. Eliminate numerical quotas
12. Remove barriers to pride of workmanship
13. Institute a vigorous program of education and retraining
14. Take action to accomplish the transformation (Deming, 1986, pp. 23–90)

JOSEPH M. JURAN

1. Build awareness of the need and opportunity for improvement
2. Set goals for improvement
3. Organize to reach the goals (establish a quality council, identify problems, select projects, appoint teams, designate a facilitator)
4. Provide training
5. Carry out projects to solve problems

6. Report progress
7. Give recognition
8. Communicate results
9. Keep score
10. Maintain momentum by making annual improvements part of the regular systems and processes of the company (Juran, 1991, p. A-10)

REFERENCES

Crosby, P. B. (1979). *Quality is free: The art of making quality certain.* New York: McGraw-Hill.

Deming, W. E. (1986). *Out of the crisis.* Cambridge, MA: Massachusetts Institute of Technology, Center for Engineering Study.

Juran, J. M. (1991). *Total quality management workshop.* Dallas, TX: U.S. Office of Personnel Management, Management Training Institute.

TQM Index
of Implementation

The "TQM Index of Implementation" is an instrument consisting of 25 Likert-type statements intended to tap the extent to which both the philosophy, principles and the methods of TQM are evident in the operations of any particular organization. It may be administered to any number of employees in an organization. Respondents should be instructed to read and reflect on each item and circle the response option which best reflects their agreement or disagreement with each item. The point of reference for the scale is provided by the introductory phase "In my organization" . . .

Scoring of the index is straight forward. "Strongly Agree" is assigned 5 points and "Strongly Disagree," 1 point, except for items 4, 12, 19 and 25 in which the scoring is reversed. The higher the score, the greater the perceived degree of implementation of TQM by the respondent.

In a 1995 study application of the TQM Index to 41 human service organizations that reported using TQM, scores ranged from a low of 54 to a high of 93 with a median of 72.

Permission to attend, use, and apply this index is freely given. Investigators may wish to experiment with the mid-point phrase of the scale by substituting "Neither Agree Nor Disagree" for "Not Applicable," for example. It would be appreciated if investigators would share their experiences with its author.

Richard Boettcher, Professor
College of Social Work, Stillman Hall
The Ohio State University
Columbus, Ohio 43210
December, 1996

TQM Index of Implementation
(Title should be removed when administered.)

Instructions: Please circle the appropriate answer under each question that best reflects your understanding of the way your organization operates. As you read each item, keep in mind the phrase, "In my Organization"...

1. Quality is our primary organizational goal.
   Strongly   Agree   Not   Disagree   Strongly
   Agree   Applicable   Disagree

2. We continually fine-tune the quality of all ourselves, even when things appear to be working well in our organization.
   Strongly   Agree   Not   Disagree   Strongly
   Agree   Applicable   Disagree

3. Clients, families, stakeholders, and other customers are active participants in determining how best to improve the quality of their products and services.
   Strongly   Agree   Not   Disagree   Strongly
   Agree   Applicable   Disagree

4. Management and professionals in the organization ultimately determine what quality is.
   Strongly   Agree   Not   Disagree   Strongly
   Agree   Applicable   Disagree

5. Customer satisfaction drives our organization.
   Strongly   Agree   Not   Disagree   Strongly
   Agree   Applicable   Disagree

6. Customers are surveyed by either using mail, telephone, or face-to-face techniques.
   Strongly   Agree   Not   Disagree   Strongly
   Agree   Applicable   Disagree

7. Citizens or communities are surveyed about services.
   Strongly   Agree   Not   Disagree   Strongly
   Agree   Applicable   Disagree

8. Customers are brought together in small groups to discuss their likes and dislikes.
   Strongly   Agree   Not   Disagree   Strongly
   Agree   Applicable   Disagree

9. Customers can make anonymous suggestions and complaints.

| Strongly Agree | Agree | Not Applicable | Disagree | Strongly Disagree |

10. Our focus in on continuous improvement.

| Strongly Agree | Agree | Not Applicable | Disagree | Strongly Disagree |

11. Change is continuous in our organization.

| Strongly Agree | Agree | Not Applicable | Disagree | Strongly Disagree |

12. Decisions are based on "gut feelings" as opposed to relying on data and analysis.

| Strongly Agree | Agree | Not Applicable | Disagree | Strongly Disagree |

13. Change is accomplished by teamwork.

| Strongly Agree | Agree | Not Applicable | Disagree | Strongly Disagree |

14. We place an emphasis on team and teamwork rather than on individual effort.

| Strongly Agree | Agree | Not Applicable | Disagree | Strongly Disagree |

15. Employees cooperate with each other.

| Strongly Agree | Agree | Not Applicable | Disagree | Strongly Disagree |

16. Departments within our organization cooperate with each other.

| Strongly Agree | Agree | Not Applicable | Disagree | Strongly Disagree |

17. Cooperation between department units is prized more than is competition.

| Strongly Agree | Agree | Not Applicable | Disagree | Strongly Disagree |

18. Managers and staff persons usually gather and analyse data on a perceived problem before actually making any changes in the way we provide our services.

| Strongly Agree | Agree | Not Applicable | Disagree | Strongly Disagree |

19. Employee training is considered a luxury.

| Strongly Agree | Agree | Not Applicable | Disagree | Strongly Disagree |

20. We have an ongoing training program so that managers and staff can learn how to do their job better.

| Strongly Agree | Agree | Not Applicable | Disagree | Strongly Disagree |

21. The flow of communication is such that everyone shares information with everyone else.

| Strongly Agree | Agree | Not Applicable | Disagree | Strongly Disagree |

22. Organizational communication is top-down, and sideways.

| Strongly Agree | Agree | Not Applicable | Disagree | Strongly Disagree |

23. Managers and supervisors are looked on as consultants who are there to ensure that staff succeed at their jobs.

| Strongly Agree | Agree | Not Applicable | Disagree | Strongly Disagree |

24. Our contractors are treated as partners, and we work cooperatively with them to provide the highest quality services possible.

| Strongly Agree | Agree | Not Applicable | Disagree | Strongly Disagree |

25. Contractors are encouraged to compete with each other on the basis of price.

| Strongly Agree | Agree | Not Applicable | Disagree | Strongly Disagree |

TQM in Human Service Organizations: A Guide to Implementation

TQM PHILOSOPHY—COMMITMENT TO CUSTOMERS

1. Briefly describe your organization and explain how it became interested in TQM.
2. What do you (management or the initiators of TQM) believe that TQM can do for your organization to improve service quality and customer satisfaction? How do you or the organization view the future as being different through TQM, in other words, did you develop or formulate a "vision statement" for your organization?
3. How do you define TQM for your organization?
4. Is your organization's approach to TQM original or an accommodation to external accreditation standards? If an accommodation, whose standards are you using?

TQM ASSESSMENT AND READINESS

1. How will you assess the readiness of your organization to implement TQM on the organizational and customer level?

2. Who will be the key players in the decision to introduce TQM to your organization? What role will they play?
3. What methods will you use to prepare your organization for TQM?
4. What kind of resistance will you experience in preparing your organization for TQM?
5. What is the nature of the understanding and commitment that workers have toward this TQM initiative?
6. What is the nature of the understanding and commitment that you have from "top" management toward this TQM initiative?
7. What kind of organizational resources are committed to this TQM initiative?

PLANNING FOR TQM

1. What organizational policies will be introduced to accommodate a shift to TQM?
2. Will the organization identify specific TQM policy objectives? What will they be?
3. Will your organization develop a plan to implement TQM? Describe the plan and how it is intended to be implemented?
4. What do you see as the strengths and weaknesses of your organization in moving toward TQM?
5. What decisions will your organization make regarding the use of consultants and training in the implementation of TQM?
6. What cost or budgetary considerations were taken into account in planning for TQM?

DEFINING CUSTOMERS

1. How will you define your internal and external customer base?
2. How will you assess customer needs? Were there specific principles that guided decisions or judgments in this area?
3. How will the quality needs of customers be factored into your organization?

ORGANIZATIONAL STRUCTURING FOR TQM

1. What initiatives will your organization take to change the organization's culture? What areas are seen as particularly critical from the perspective of this TQM's initiative?

2. How will customers play a part in restructuring policy-making authority and control in your organization?
3. What strategies will be used to reorganize work tasks and initiate problem-solving activities in your organization?
4. How will your organization coordinate the multiple service functions of your organization?
5. Will your organization achieve service integration among the various program components of your organization?

EMPLOYEE EMPOWERMENT

1. What part will employee training and education play in this TQM initiative?
2. How will teams be developed within your organization?
3. Will teams be composed of members from all levels of the organization or from the same level(s) of the organization?
4. What are the organizational barriers that your organization has to overcome to implement teams?
5. How will your organization coordinate the work of the various teams?

SERVICE DELIVERY PROCESSING

1. What work processes will be implemented to ensure the delivery of quality services?
2. What will be the primary service technologies used in the delivery of services to your customers?
3. How will your organization ensure reliability, access, responsiveness, competence, credibility, and courtesy to customers?

CONTINUOUS QUALITY IMPROVEMENT

1. What procedures will be developed to ensure CQI in the management of finances, time, and human resources?
2. What procedures will be developed to ensure CQI within the various units and divisions of your organizations, in other words, interorganizational considerations.

STATISTICAL MONITORING

1. What measures will be introduced to determine progress in the direction of quality improvement? How are these measures to be introduced and implemented?
2. Has your organization viewed statistical monitoring as relevant to the solution of service "quality" problems?
3. How will your organization use statistical methodology in monitoring CQI?
4. What part will statistical monitoring play in determining levels of customer satisfaction?
5. Are any qualitative measures being used in this TQM initiative?

QUALITY TRAINING AND EDUCATION

1. What resources are available to invest in quality training and education?
2. What philosophies, concepts, and principles do you wish to include in your educational efforts?
3. What applied skills do you wish to emphasize in your training?
4. How will you evaluate your training and education function?
5. How will you provide for continuous training and education?

Feedback Survey

Please fill out this survey so that CQI can be made by the authors of *Making TQM Work: Quality Tools for Human Service Organizations.* Postage will be paid by the addressee.

1. What value did this book have for you? Please explain as fully as possible.

_____

_____

_____

_____

_____

_____

_____

_____

2. Which tools did you find most helpful? Please explain.

_____

_____

_____

_____

_____

_____

_____

_____

3. What changes and/or additions would you suggest?

_____

_____

_____

_____

_____

_____

_____

_____

Thank you.

Index